James McNeish [illegible]ght and biographer [illegible]ew Zealand and abroad. Born in Auckland in 1931, as a young man he travelled the world, working as a deckhand on a Norwegian freighter, in the theatre in London and as a journalist for the BBC, *Guardian* and *Observer.*

He received many awards and fellowships, including the New Zealand Prime Minister's Award for literary achievement in non-fiction in 2010. He was made a Knight Companion of the New Zealand Order of Merit the following year.

Also by James McNeish

NON-FICTION

Tavern in the Town

Fire under the Ashes

Larks in a Paradise (with Marti Friedlander)

As for the Godwits

Art of the Pacific (with Brian Brake)

Belonging

Walking on My Feet (with Helen McNeish)

Ahnungslos in Berlin

The Man from Nowhere and Other Prose

The Mask of Sanity

An Albatross Too Many

Dance of the Peacocks

The Sixth Man

Touchstone

FICTION

Mackenzie

The Mackenzie Affair

The Glass Zoo

Joy

Lovelock

Penelope's Island

My Name is Paradiso

Mr Halliday and the Circus Master

The Crime of Huey Dunstan

BREAKING RANKS

JAMES McNEISH

HarperCollinsPublishers

HarperCollins*Publishers*

First published in 2017
by HarperCollins*Publishers* (New Zealand) Limited
Unit D1, 63 Apollo Drive, Rosedale, Auckland 0632, New Zealand
harpercollins.co.nz

HarperCollins*Publishers*
Unit D1, 63 Apollo Drive, Rosedale, Auckland 0632, New Zealand
Level 13, 201 Elizabeth Street, Sydney NSW 2000, Australia
A 53, Sector 57, Noida, UP, India
1 London Bridge Street, London, SE1 9GF, United Kingdom
2 Bloor Street East, 20th floor, Toronto, Ontario M4W 1A8, Canada
195 Broadway, New York NY 10007, USA

A catalogue record for this book is available from
the National Library of New Zealand

ISBN 978 1 7755 4090 8 (pbk)
ISBN 978 1 7754 9127 9 (ebook)

Cover design by Hazel Lam, HarperCollins Design Studio
Cover images by shutterstock.com
Typeset in Sabon LT by Kirby Jones
Printed and bound in Australia by Griffin Press
The papers used by HarperCollins in the manufacture of this book are a natural, recyclable product made from wood grown in sustainable plantation forests. The fibre source and manufacturing processes meet recognised international environmental standards, and carry certification.

CONTENTS

Wer spricht von Siegen? Überstehen ist alles.
(Who speaks of victories? To endure is all.)

Rainer Maria Rilke, *Requiem*

This book is about three men who defied authority, and paid for it. A doctor, a soldier and a judge. Each was at the top of his profession. The title and subtitle of this book suggest a continuity, and, indeed, as I researched and wrote the stories, certain events and incidents I didn't know about emerged, suggesting a creatively neater approach built around a unified or common theme. But although each life is the stuff of fiction and the three share a common fate, dying prematurely when they had so much to give, more separates their stories than unites them. I have therefore resisted the novelist's approach and the urge to fictionalise their stories, preferring to let each life stand alone as a story in its own right.

Having said that, I have been conscious when writing this book of a remark some forty years ago by the art critic and teacher, Eric McCormick. He said, 'Have you ever noticed the anarchic streak in this society?' I hadn't. I had never thought about it. He didn't elaborate. Nor do I recall what triggered McCormick's remark. It might have been something quite simple, like the well-known episode when Kiwi troops in Libya failed to salute Field Marshal Montgomery, who then complained to Freyberg, who said, 'I'm sure if you give 'em a wave, sir, they'll wave back.' Or the occasion when Joe Heenan, Secretary for Internal Affairs, left his cheese-cutter on a hook at Buckingham Palace after departing from a royal row.

Over the years I have come to realise that there is more than a grain of truth in McCormick's remark. But this is the first time in my experience that an element of anarchy — the heretical streak in our makeup — has invaded the page unasked, as a kind of back story or mutinous subtext. In this sense the three essays, although quite separate, are not entirely random. All three men defy convention in a way that goes beyond mere dissent. A streak of subversion lingers.

Three lives, then; three provocateurs, innovators and visionaries, who died before their time. Two destroy themselves, and the third — betrayal, it is said, being more dependable than friendship — dies in furious sorrow. Not all three are born New Zealanders. Yet the doctor, who is English and who might be called in the language of fifty years ago a new-New Zealander, is arguably more than that, having transcended definition by being honoured on his deathbed by local tangata whenua and beyond.

Finally, I note that I have changed names in two or three instances at the subject's request, to protect privacy.

JOHN SAXBY

Sometimes after a good dinner and some wine my wife and I will sit around the table afterwards and talk about absent friends. 'Who is it we miss most?' Helen will say. Invariably, almost as inevitable as the next sunrise, one name will come up, that of John Saxby: the only person she claims to have stayed in our house for any length of time who was unobtrusive to the point of near-invisibility. John spent three weeks with us in Wellington in the early nineties. He had designed an outbuilding, a Japanese tea-house, for me to write in and insisted on coming down to help me build it. What I remember about the visit is his gaiety; he was an uncomplicated and benign guest.

He turns up, or is reputed to turn up, in a novel by Brigid Brophy, *The King of a Rainy Country*, as the young man who is hanging about in the kitchen forever eating cornflakes. I said to John, 'What do you have for breakfast?'

'Cornflakes usually,' he said.

I saw him in action in a professional capacity only once. At the rural institution on the edge of the King Country where he worked in the Waikato, he was holding a discussion session with a group of young patients. I sat in and listened. It was the first time we had met, following an introduction by telephone, and this was a different person altogether from the one who came to stay in 1991. Here was no benign house guest but a masquerading Pierrot, grotesque and impish as one of those gnomes you see as gargoyles, water-spouting from the walls of gothic churches in Italy. John was protean. I knew nothing of his earlier self, or selves: the actor in him, the poet, the translator, the oarsman, the mountaineer, or the innovator and alchemist in the field of mental disorders. Or any of his other selves in a past life. Only a few shards from that brilliant personality were beamed in my direction. At Tokanui Psychiatric Hospital, he was engaged as a psychiatrist, working under Henry Bennett. After Dr Bennett retired as medical superintendent of the hospital in 1984, John succeeded him. And then, nine years later, John died.

Ours was not an intense friendship, although it was intimate and real. We met only intermittently, with long gaps in between. I was often away, sometimes a year at a time. We met perhaps ten or fifteen times in twenty years. Yet such was his gift for friendship that I feel, looking back, that I have been under his spell for a whole lifetime.

In 1994, the year after John died, I was in London having dinner with Derek Robinson, a paediatrician who had known John at Oxford. We were talking about this and that. The members' dining room at the Royal Society of Medicine in Wimpole Street was busy but pleasantly relaxed. A man sitting alone a couple of tables away sent a note across to Derek. It said, 'Do we know each other?'

To which Derek answered, 'Yes.' When the other man joined us, Derek said to him, 'We were talking about a mutual acquaintance in New Zealand. This is James McNeish. Did you know John Saxby?'

'My God,' said the other man. 'He used to climb up the stonework into my room. Who *didn't* know Saxby!'

The other man turned out to be someone Derek had been wanting to contact for an anniversary gaudy at Oxford, a surgeon named Mann. Charles Mann and Derek Robinson had been undergraduates at New College in 1947, after the war, but hadn't met again in the forty-seven years since. They were two of perhaps only three or four contemporaries of John Saxby at New College who had taken medicine in the immediate postwar years. So it was that I began to piece together in a haphazard way some of his history.

* * *

John had described his parents to me, his father especially, as somewhat odd. The father was without a trade but had become a businessman. He made widgets. He designed component parts, and bits of machinery and gadgets to wind springs and drill holes or make angles which had no history and no name. In the war the army engaged him on secret work, making gadgets for things by the million.

'My dear Miles,' he said to a friend, 'you cannot imagine how many a million is.'

The friend, Miles Vaughan Williams, was another doctor I met. We met in a rainstorm outside Hertford College, of which Dr Vaughan Williams, a distant cousin of the composer, was a fellow. He used to visit the Saxbys in Abingdon, he said, where the father, Oliver, had his workshop in a rambling house where, I assumed, wrongly as it turned out, that John was born. Vaughan Williams described Oliver Saxby as an amateur bloke, 'quite unlettered'. He told me that when John's mother became ill and immobile, confined to her bedroom, Oliver designed a travelling chair with a harness, and built a monorail at ceiling height, so she was able to get about the house from room to room independently, under her own steam.

'Oliver was an absolute wizard,' Vaughan Williams said. 'We nabbed him for the Department of Pharmacology here in Oxford. He liked things being broken. "Good," he'd say, and rub his hands. "Now I can fix it." He liked addressing problems where other people hadn't been before. You say John was an innovator? He probably got it from the father by osmosis.'

Which may help to explain the significance of our first meeting in New Zealand, the group discussion I attended at Tokanui. The year was 1970 or perhaps earlier, John having arrived from England with his wife and four children in 1966. He had invited me to Tokanui at my request (I was researching a play). The discussion I attended took place in an open ward. The participants were inmates, all voluntary, almost all Pakeha. They exhibited a variety of behavioural and mental disorders, he told me, largely undiagnosed. They sat on chairs in a semi-circle; John squatted in the centre. He wore a rumpled fawn suit, and led a discussion that was lively and at one point became so personal and edgy, with gales of laughter and insults flying — mostly in his direction — that I wanted to hide. John seemed impervious. His ears became pointed, that was all. He parried the insults and became so caught up in the discussion that he was indistinguishable from the rest. An outsider would not have known he wasn't one of the patients.

What I was witnessing was an experiment in group therapy. In retrospect, it can be seen as a blueprint: the genesis of a socio-psychiatric movement that would spread through New Zealand and see psychotherapy brought into the institutions. Put differently, it was the beginning of a more humanist approach to the treatment of mental illness in New Zealand, helping to rid our asylums of the stigma of cruelty so vividly described in Janet Frame's autobiographical novel, *Owls Do Cry*. At Tokanui, John was working alone.

How or why he came from England I have never discovered, except anecdotally. He appears to have been sent down from the British Army or some other august body, in the way one was sent down at the time from the University of Oxford, 'for unspecified offences', meaning a contravention of the moral code. As indeed happened to his contemporary and friend, the writer Brigid Brophy, a confessed bisexual, who was thrown out of Oxford for breaking the rules, and with whom he may have been, I suspect, at one time in love. Nor did I discover why — since he wasn't very good at it and would undoubtedly have shone in another profession like architecture — he chose medicine, unless it was to do with his father.

'In my Father's house,' we read in John's Gospel, chapter 14, 'are many mansions.' Certainly John's father was many-sided. Before becoming a whiz at widgets, Oliver Baber Saxby had been a magistrate. A decent, charming and liberal human being, by all accounts, he nonetheless believed, according to Miles Vaughan Williams, in the sanctity of corporal punishment.

'Ra-ther! Young louts, give 'em a good flogging. Ra-ra-ra.' When flogging was abolished, Oliver resigned from the Bench. 'I'm not going to have these young thugs coming in and being handed out lollipops and candy. Birching, that's what's needed. If we can't flog 'em, I'm going.' So he resigned. He took rather the same attitude towards John. They didn't get on. They had some hard words. You can imagine the rest.

John was an only child and, according to his wife, Felicity, a lonely child, sent away to boarding school in Bedford at the age of eight. He liked science and was good at sketching things and designing houses; he had an inquisitive mind bordering on the exotic, and perhaps, as with the neurologist Oliver Sacks, there was a touch of genius as well. Oliver Sacks is the doctor who emigrated from England to America and wrote *The Man Who Mistook His Wife for a Hat.* Sacks and Saxby? Both were *humane* clinicians. That means they preferred patients to laboratories, people to potions, human waywardness to technical certainties. That's rarer than you think. Both grew up shy with a desire to show off, and were drawn to pursuits involving risk and danger. They are alike in many ways. Oliver Sacks rode motor-bikes, went to Canada to join the air force and became a neurologist by accident; John Saxby climbed mountains and followed a similar roundabout route into medicine. However the similarities are mostly superficial. Oliver the father may have pushed John into doctoring; on the other hand, the son may have grasped at it in subconscious rebellion to a cane-wielding father.

Derek Robinson says, 'He was an idealist. Medicine appealed to him — even though he wasn't very good at it — as part of the broader humanities. I mean, he took the Oath seriously. That part of the Oath which talks of warmth and human sympathy and understanding "outweighing the surgeon's knife" was pure Saxby. Almost a biblical text for him. Though, funnily enough, he'd have made a good surgeon. John was good on canals and bones, the topography of the human body. But bad on physiology and diseases, like me. We both had difficulty passing exams.

'I have a mental picture of him in a corridor, leaning back against the wall talking to someone, a patient, and listening. White coat hanging down, his hands pressed in a mitre against his chest, fingers touching, nodding and listening. He was always listening. He wanted to know everything.

'We did a stint together at Westminster as housemen. Then came Suez, but I'd lost touch with him by then. After Suez the army claimed him.' If life is a progression of chance, John's life is a classic example, even if he did grow up conditioned by institutions (school, university, hospital) pointing to a conventional career. What appealed was risk and danger, elements the army would soon supply in abundance.

Derek pictures a young doctor who takes the stories of patients as subjective truths. I see him already a student drawn to trauma among his contemporaries, which may sound implausible until you remember that many of his fellow students at New College in 1946–47 were soldiers in civvies who had just been discharged. Here he was, a tender schoolboy of seventeen; and here were all these warriors in their thirties coming back from the war. The average age in the junior common room in Trinity term at New College that year, we read, according to the three-volume *History of Oxford*, was twenty-eight. Ex-majors with Military Crosses, wives and moustaches 'had little in common with seventeen-year-old boys who carried green ration books entitling them to extra bananas'. However, in the case of a listener like John, the interlocutor incarnate, there was a commonality and merging of interests. And the key was milk, not bananas.

'I liked purveyors of fire and horror stories,' he told me once. 'I could draw people out. At New College I earned a brief fame. It was on account of the milk. As a minor, I was allowed a double ration at the buttery. The milk introduced me to a wider circle of friends than I'd otherwise have had. These army chaps, some of them almost old enough to be my father, would come to me for coffee or invite me to coffee because I had the wherewithal to go with it.'

John's rooms at New College were high up a staircase. He became adept at negotiating the perpendicular walls, climbing up the Victorian gothic pile to get into his rooms late at night after the gates were locked. 'He showed me how to go up a drainpipe and down the other side,' a contemporary says. 'He did it all the time.

He was fantastically strong in the shoulders.' It came from rowing — not in the eights, but in the single sculls. But rock-climbing was the real passion, because of the enhanced risk.

We all take risks, have a hidden wish to show off and be thought well of. A secret urge to assert ourselves and be rewarded? A leap to save a drowning child? It's generally a spur-of-the-moment thing. But it's also a matter of temperament: a form of exhibitionism. A desire to shock in the young may be harmless juvenilia, or it may mask other forms of behaviour like a lack of instinct for self-preservation which will recur in adult life and which may not be quite so harmless. Who knows?

In the army John was, as a doctor, automatically made an officer. He would acknowledge the salute of other ranks on the parade ground with a cheery 'Hello'. A mild enough tic, perhaps, but it infuriated the drill sergeant. A sense of the absurd seems always to have been there.

After graduating he took a house job at the Middlesex in central London. Nurses and staff arriving one day on the early shift were surprised to find a galaxy of figures peering down at them from the façade of the hospital in Wimpole Street. They were gnomes. They wore night-caps. They were cemented on and around the ledges and porticos, decorating the face of the building. They were fishing, their lines depending from little rods into the hospital yard just behind Oxford Street. John, it was explained to me by an eyewitness, had a prankish side.

Call it grandstanding. It was also perhaps a saving grace, a way of handling a kink of nature in response to a humdrum world. It was an aspect of his persona that would appeal to people in trouble and help make him such a good therapist.

* * *

I think Suez helped. It tested him. Nobody born after 1950 can be expected to remember the crisis which marked Britain's fall as a world power — the moment when the prime minister, Anthony Eden, made the mistake of invading Egypt in an attempt to topple its president, Gamal Nasser, after he nationalised the Suez Canal in 1956. As a war game involving misunderstandings and idiocies that misfired, it recalls the Charge of the Light Brigade at Balaclava, and is almost as colourful.

The story is told of a journalist who acquired a certain amount of opprobrium. He turned up in John's battalion, having put it around that he'd been a captain in the territorials, and a seasoned paratrooper. He was duly invited and made welcome in the battalion mess. One day he found himself in a queue, third from the front, lining up to draw a parachute for the invasion. Next to him was an Irish sergeant, Paddy Durham. The journalist turned to Paddy and confessed he'd never jumped in his life. 'If you don't mind, I think I'll miss this one,' he said. Paddy considered for a minute, then said: 'You're fucking coming.' They gave him a parachute and took him up in the plane and threw him out of the aircraft. In the air he blacked out. He landed on the runway in Port Said and was one of John's first casualties of the invasion.[1]

John was a young married man, attached as medical officer to the Third Battalion, the only British unit in the combined Anglo-French invasion force which jumped. He was reluctant to talk about it, but he did say that when first conscripted for his national service he put in for commandos.

'They have tests,' he related, 'designed to weed out people who cannot cope on their own. For instance they say "Sit down", "Run to that wall and back". Anyone who

1 The journalist was patched up and his story duly appeared in London. It was headlined 'I jumped with the paras'. It earned him a commendation and he became a hero.

spins around and doesn't do one or the other gets chucked. There are no failures. I was worried by the assault course. My worry was I wouldn't get through, which would have meant being parted from my wife. It would have meant my being sent to Kyoto, to a general hospital in Japan. Wives weren't allowed. So I volunteered for the Parachute Brigade which superseded all other options.'

And then, Suez. He talked about it to me only once, slightingly, in a mock-heroic Oxford way. How they were first camped out among the olive and orange groves of Cyprus, the transit point for the invasion. The airfields jam-packed with transport and bomber planes. He described the days of anxious waiting. Of coping with a hot, dusty wind which covered their kit with a sandy film 'as cloying as cocoa powder'. Of eating breakfast crammed down in the midnight hours and boarding a troopship in Famagusta harbour, only to be taken off in favour of a sapper unit amid the confusion and chaos of last-minute changes caused by the decision to land the paras 24 hours ahead of the seaborne assault. Most of this, I've got from books. John wouldn't talk about it.

The task of the paras, I learned, was to seize and secure the airfield at Port Said. The runway was beside the town's sewerage system. It was flanked by marshes, and Egyptian soldiers dug in along the beaches and behind pillboxes, armed with rockets and other weapons supplied by Soviet Russia. John said little of the drop itself, or the funk fears as they flew towards Egypt, scared not only of what awaited them but scared of being scared, and of being seen to be scared.

'There was no live rehearsal,' I remember him saying. 'It was a bit of a guddle.' I remember that, too. So much of life was like that, a guddle, as he liked to say, a shambles or a cock-up. I pointed out that a dry run for an invasion nobody was supposed to know about until it happened might be difficult. He agreed. How could you be expected to taste in advance the flavour of jumping out of an aeroplane at night in a 35-mile-per-hour gale while being shot at? Or envisage red and green tracer arching towards you as you floated earthwards? Or hear your first mortar bomb, bullets 'cracking all over the place' and, from time to time, balls of fire tearing along the runway chasing the soles of your boots as you staggered about trying to unload your gear.

Roy Fullick I met in London. He was one of those who jumped at Suez and was happy to talk. He described John in a voice of mild censure, tinged I thought with admiration, as 'a soldier all to himself'.

'I didn't know him very well and I didn't see much of him after we landed,' said Roy, who was a major in command of a company in the Third Battalion. 'We had these huge loads, one hundred pounds in the case of the medical officer. The kitbags were released as you jumped, attached to your leg by a rope. It was very difficult to unpack your gear; you had first to get rid of your collapsed 'chute before you could get at the container for your weapons in the kitbag. I was making for the tower. It was impossible to run more than a few yards. The last I saw of John, he was weaving about with this enormous load looking for someone to link up with from the surgical team. They started patching up the casualties even before the fighting on the airfield was over.'

The experience, he thought, had meant a great deal to John. It led to a prolonged stint at Netley near Southampton, where he joined a military psychiatric unit. Like the Scottish psychiatrist, R.D. Laing, John was finding in the army an interest in communicating with victims of stress. It marked a change of direction in his life, which would lead ten years later to his arrival at Tokanui.

* * *

He never talked about Suez. 'Not to me,' Felicity said, 'not to the children, not to anyone.' To me, it was just the once. The occasion was fortuitous, the result of an incident when he came to stay with us in Wellington.

I met him at the airport. He flew down from Hamilton bearing a window and nothing else except a small bag no bigger than the Gladstone bag I used to take my lunch in to grammar school. It was a rose cottage window. He'd found it in a junk yard in Te Awamutu. We duly installed the window in the tea-house we were building on a hill behind our house. It looked down onto an arm of Wellington harbour.

All went well until one morning when we began nailing down the deck, which was cantilevered over a gully. Below was a sheer drop. John was on the edge, facing me, hammering away. One minute he was there, the next not. I looked down. Far below, screened by a tracery of bramble and rose thorns, lay a crumpled figure, quite still. I thought, *This is unreal.* For a moment I thought he was dead. I called out. Silence. Then I heard a muffled grunt. He seemed to shake himself. The next minute he had climbed the steps and was beside me again, hammering away as if nothing had happened.

'My God,' I said, 'how did you learn to fall like that? Are you all right?'

He said, 'Perfectly, thank you.' It was then he told me he'd been a paratrooper and how they teach you to fall without hurting yourself. I was persuaded to draw him out a little.

I was writing a novel based on a real-life New Zealander who had parachuted into occupied Greece in the Second World War. I wanted to know what it was like to jump. I asked. He obliged at once.

'The man who sends you is called the despatcher. Two despatchers actually, one on each side of you. "Red on, stand in the doors. Go!" And you hear "Go! Go! Go!" A doorless opening is the most satisfactory. There are fewer snarl-ups. But in a thirty-five-mile-an-hour gale you're going to break a lot of legs ...' And so on.

I used John's words in the novel, almost verbatim. They were too good to be untrue. When the book was published, friends came up to me and said, in some astonishment, 'Where did *you* learn to parachute?' I said I hadn't, that I'd never jumped off anything higher than a wooden horse in a gymnasium. But they refused to believe me.

I think John would have been pleased to see himself in print, had he lived. The book was called *My Name is Paradiso.* I hadn't looked at it for years until I took it down the other day, when I was writing this chapter. I had forgotten the date it was published — it appeared in 1995, 18 months after John had died. I had forgotten, too, the dedication:

To
John Saxby
for a quarter of a century,
in memory

* * *

Tokanui when John arrived in the 1960s was one of a dozen mental health institutions in New Zealand which had to a greater or lesser degree a history involving the stigma of abuse or mental cruelty. Conditions were primitive. Disruptive patients were locked away in seclusion and out of sight; for patients with rampant delusions and hallucinations, drug therapy involving intra-muscular injections of phenothiazine medication like Modecate was normal and acceptable. There was a lack of trained staff, and hence supervision; physical abuse, ECT or electric shock treatment, and lobotomies (surgical brain incisions for supposedly 'intractable' mental disorders) were common, and commonly misdiagnosed, as in the case of Janet Frame.

Janet Frame was hospitalised at the Seacliff Lunatic Asylum near Dunedin for several periods in the 1950s. She was then a young woman and unknown in the literary world. She was first diagnosed as suffering from schizophrenia. She was given electroconvulsive therapy and insulin. When this failed to benefit her, her mother was persuaded to sign a letter of consent for a brain operation which in all probability would have left her daughter a vegetable. She was rescued at the last moment when, three days before the operation was due to be performed, it was announced that she had won the Hubert Church Memorial Award for prose, at that time the country's highest literary award. The scheduled lobotomy was cancelled.

In England in her novel *Mrs Dalloway* (1925), Virginia Woolf had tackled the theme in an attempt to portray schizophrenia. But it would be Janet Frame's exploration of her perilous descent into mental distress and 'madness' over years of hospitalisation, in *Owls Do Cry*, published in 1957, that would prove to be a landmark as one of the first works of fiction to portray life in a mental institution.

That said, there is no guarantee that had Janet Frame been admitted to Tokanui instead of Seacliff her diagnosis and treatment would have been radically different. The possibility, however, seems remote; and after the charismatic Henry Bennett took over in 1964, almost non-existent.

Henry Rongomau Bennett was a tall, imposing man, but of the old school. He was the first Maori medical superintendent of a mental health institution. One of the first things he did on taking over at Tokanui was remove the 'institutional' look. He began by demolishing a three-metre-high mesh fence behind the forensic block, known as The Pen ('pen' for 'penitentiary'), and cutting down trees and hedges which had grown up, hiding and isolating the wards. He was much criticised; staff threatened to resign; patients, they said, would abscond, run away, commit crimes. But they didn't (and the few who ran off were collected and brought back by the locals). Tokanui, built on swamp and marshland originally to take the overflow from other mental institutions, started to breathe more easily. When John Saxby arrived, he found in contrast to some English institutions that he'd known, not to mention Dunedin's Seacliff whose gothic façade with rooms locked and barred was emblematic of lunacy, that he was entering what appeared to be an open park.

There were no security fences. He found instead a cluster of wooden houses and two-storey ward villas set in a panorama of gardens and lanes of deciduous trees, elms and birches and oaks, spread over 110 acres. Adjoining the grounds were a further 1000 acres of farmland belonging to the hospital, where patients worked, tending pigs and milking cows. The hospital was home to almost a thousand souls, from the feeble-minded to the acutely demented, some referred on from a reformatory prison — Waikeria — which was just up the road. There was still physical restraint; electro-convulsive shock treatment was used; inquisitive news reporters had no trouble in finding patients they described as 'bewildered and frightened'. That was one reality. Another was of a self-contained village with its own bakery and laundry, which had been providing jobs for entire families for generations. Another was that 60 per cent of the patient population was voluntary. Still another was the absence of qualified psychiatrists, a reflection of the fact that very few clinical psychiatrists existed in the country at all.

For many years, it was explained to me, John and one other colleague were the only two staff members 'not to have been previously patients'. There were doctors on the staff, it was further explained, 'who were either giving an ECT or being given an ECT'.

For someone of John's temperament, Tokanui's hit-or-miss atmosphere wasn't a bad thing. He had an insatiable curiosity; he wasn't afraid of work; he enjoyed difficulties.

Intractable mental states were food and drink to him, the more curious the better. Faced with a mosaic of human frailties and unresolved neurological oddities, he had if nothing else considerable room to manoeuvre.

Another way of looking at it is the Lone Piper factor, first remarked on by a nineteen-year-old trainee from Dunedin, Geraldine Keith. Near the entrance to the hospital was a knoll or mound, a small distinctive hill on top of which Geraldine noticed, if the weather was fine and sometimes even when it wasn't, a solitary figure would appear, playing the bagpipes.

Her experience up to then had been a studentship at Cherry Farm, where she had looked after a ward of about fifty women, who spent much of the day in the day room — 'stonked out', with their heads back.

'I used to take them soup. They never saw a visitor, ever. Tokanui, by contrast, was another world. People were active. It was already an approach towards a more perfect community.

'It never seemed odd that this lone piper should walk through the grounds playing his pipes whenever he felt like it, he was part of it. He was respected and honoured in the community. I do mean honoured. When he was on his mound, he was Braveheart.'

This was the sixties still. The Saxbys hadn't long arrived.

'I liked the gait and grammar of the place,' John told me. 'You could move from top to bottom without difficulties. Sure, we had locked doors and restraints in acute admissions. There had to be. But you could connect everywhere.'

Tokanui was still an old-fashioned unsanitary institution, yet to be prised out of its Victorian past. Old staff nurses recall John's bewilderment on arrival; others his restlessness and energy, which were a driving force from the start.

'He had an uncanny power [one ex-nurse says] to re-diagnose and motivate people. "Tell me," he'd say to a depressive who had ended up in the wrong ward, "what on earth brings you here?" He had a way of getting on side with the patient.' As with the lone piper, who appears to have been a chronic schizophrenic. Another patient he befriended went about talking to an imaginary parrot on his shoulder.

'He'd always say hello and stop for a chat. The word "abnormal" was not in his vocabulary.'

But this was later. First, he built a house.

* * *

He bought a piece of land beside Te Mawhai Road, passing the hospital, further down but near enough to be able to walk to work. On it he put a house built to his own design that was abnormal. It was an Italian-type villa with wooden shutters, severely rectangular. There was a short driveway. Where it left the road, he planted a magnolia tree and a wintersweet which overhung and partly obscured the driveway. The latter was artfully pruned so that to get by, brushing against it, you carried the lemony scent with you to the front door.

The house was unpainted. You invariably drove past and missed it. He had a disregard for anything that interfered with the environment. The exterior remained grey, the opposite of his personality. Its austerity such — no gables, finials, corbels, projections of any kind to disturb its flat exterior and the beautifully proportioned windows — that it appeared based on no known principles of architecture. I suspect it owed something to the innovations of the seventeenth-century English architect, Inigo Jones. But on one level John had raised the house up, thus leaping a couple of hundred years to Italian classical, popular in England until the end of the nineteenth century.

He had persuaded his neighbour to plant a tree, a birch or claret ash, in an open field so he could lie in the bath with a pot of tea at his elbow and see it through the downstairs window. Indeed, almost all of the rooms were designed to capture this tree and the panorama beyond, opening out to Mount Pirongia and its neighbour Kakepuku in the west. This was possible because the design incorporated a ha-ha, which hid the neighbour's electric fence and allowed an unimpeded view of the Pirongia landscape.

The first time Geraldine Keith stayed in the house, John made a point of introducing her to the boiler downstairs. 'Every time I went down I'd have to say hello to the boiler.

'He designed the house to his own specifications to the last millimetre. I asked him once if he'd like to change anything. "Yes," he said, after a long pause, hand on chin, "the handles on the French doors."'

Upstairs was a room, long and airy, with a floor of pitch pine. There was a nook, with wooden seats, as you entered from the hall. I remember my first visit — kitchen odours, the music of Shostakovich, and a pleasing disarray of objects, pictures, books, record albums, irradiated by delicate tints and whorls of dust reflected in the west window. The room seemed to stretch the length of a picture gallery. It contained hidden spaces and echoes, faint sounds which turned out to be the *pop-pop* of a distant train coming through the window like the touch of soft, busy hands. In a corner hidden by a haze of cigarette smoke sat Felicity, bent over a jigsaw puzzle.

A house, he liked to say, was simply a way of organising space which should be ambiguous and thus versatile. He was perhaps advancing a portrait of himself. His house was a door into a fuller life, which, with the calls on his time and the Braun bleeper that he wore clipped to his pocket, became an extension of the hospital itself, almost an out-clinic. It was also a refuge and a citadel where he hid himself away, listened to music, wrote verse and translated Rilke from the German. After the children grew up and left home, he converted a neighbour's cottage into a workshop and built things with his hands, although his restlessness and urge to create did not extend to gardening. He refused to garden. There was, however, a tomato house, which in 1981 was inhabited by members of the Mongrel Mob. This was during the Springbok Tour when John and Felicity were in the front-line of the field invasion which stopped the game in Hamilton. Afterwards they were besieged by almost daily threats. Patients from B Ward and a mobster and his mates camped in the house and grounds in relays, to ensure the Saxbys were not molested.

Not all of the staff at the hospital loved him, it must be said. Colleagues in the profession considered him aloof or a show-off. To many he was an anomaly. Basil James, the national director of Mental Health, who was both friend and admirer, thought he was wasting his time labouring in the fields among bucolic minds, when he might have been better employed in an intellectually challenging academic environment. Many misunderstood him in this way.

'I am an idealist,' he was not afraid of saying. Few understood the depths of his romanticism, which was essentially a desire to make himself useful. If he laboured amid the downtrodden and the rejected, it was by choice. And the house he built reflected this.

The house was a symbol, a statement of intent. He had found the place he was looking for. I am reminded of a story he told about the guy who was playing the violin but always played only the one note. Just the one, time after time. Chap in the flat upstairs, he finally went and banged on the door. 'Other people,' he said, 'when they play the violin, they go up and down and they make different notes.' 'No, no,' the guy said, 'they're looking for the right place. I've *found* it.'

I think he built it for eternity. He never named the house. He had no wish to be remembered. What is surprising is the picture you get today from people who must have been quite junior at the time, young nurses and therapists, and who remember— What? Well. They remember the ha-ha.

And the goats he kept. They remember the wisteria by the west window, the artfully pruned wintersweet in the driveway, the sign in the television room (*Please do not sit on the baby*). They remember him coming to the door, bleeper in one hand, a cup of tea in the other, greeting them with the hint of a frown and a mop of hair falling over his brow. They remember the crocheted coverlets in the big room, and the Andrew Wyeth painting on the wall of the downstairs bedroom, *Christina's World*. They must have come often. I think he liked making himself available. The house gave them, Felicity said, some of their happiest years.

At the end he took himself off to Kashmir, of all places, adding yet another layer to the enigma of his death.

After John died, Maros Hollóköi, a young Hungarian who became John's registrar and lived in the house when he went to Kashmir, gave me a list of John's pet likes and dislikes, which took up most of a three-page letter. 'He liked drinking flat beer', Maros wrote. 'He used to invite me over in the evenings sometimes to listen to Shostakovich. I remember him washing up in the kitchen listening to Shostakovich, and the rhythm of a passing train.'

'He used to make the most wonderful brew of tea,' Maros said. It was always a blend of two, three or more teas, spooned into the pot.

* * *

One morning, one of the staff on duty in Admissions, Rachel, looked out and saw the boss approaching, walking to work through the trees with his particular gait, as usual. But before reaching the path leading to his office in Admissions, he turned off in the direction of Ward 7. This was not particularly unusual.

'Dr Saxby would arrive about eight-thirty. You'd see him striding through the trees, sometimes with Rosie, his dog, trotting beside him. Sometimes he'd head for Rehab in Villa 7 or call in at B Ward, but this time it was Ward 7. Same thing, next day.'

Rachel guessed he was probably checking on Andrew, one of the new arrivals. Andrew was a borderline schizophrenic, yet undiagnosed. A difficult one, Andrew. He'd come in as so many did, off the streets. Difficult, because of the drugs.

'Dr Saxby was very good at not medicating, if he could help it. He'd worry. Sometimes the work and the overall responsibility got on top of him. He'd worry himself sick if he couldn't get it right first time — the diagnosis, I mean — in the case of a manic depressive or a query schizo like Andrew. If there was the slightest glimmer of hope, of not having to medicate the guy and whack drugs into him, that's the way he'd go. He had these *huge* expectations of himself. He had to get it right. The difficulty with Andrew was that he was very negative. Somebody sent him to us. He arrived blotto.'

That isn't quite how Andrew remembers it. Andrew Stone was 22 at the time, and a mature student. He recalls being picked off the streets in Auckland and sent first to Carrington Hospital; then nothing, until he was transferred to Tokanui. He thinks his mother must have arranged it through friends in Hamilton. Andrew was hallucinating.

'I was seeing visions. People were calling to me. I was hearing voices all the time, day and night, without realising what was happening to me.'

He arrived perplexed, with a particular aversion to drug therapy, and ready to bolt, Andrew says. The doctor who saw him sat with his hands pointed under his chin and said nothing, then asked him to go outside and walk about under the trees. When Andrew returned, the doctor was still sitting in the same position with his hands pressed to his chin like a mitre. 'Suddenly he shouted for a pen. "A pen, a pen! Why doesn't someone give me a pen in this godforsaken place!" I thought this peculiar, especially as he had a pen sticking out of his pocket. He wrote down what I said on the back of an envelope, which he folded in half, then told me what they had to offer: group classes and group discussions, a swimming pool if I liked swimming. I liked him, but I was quite negative. I just wanted to be on my way.'

After a little time in Ward 7, Andrew was transferred to another ward, where he took his medication and sweated it out. 'I was hanging out for a cigarette. A kind old lady gave me a packet of cigarettes. The doctor came to see me. "Call me John," he said. He said this to everyone. I mentioned what I was trying to do in my line of work and my political convictions. He listened and made notes. I overheard him say to some of the staff, "It's not what happens, it's *who* it happens to." He then arranged for me to be transferred to Ward 21A. This was incredibly understanding of him. I'd seen the clients of 21A out in the sun, dancing to music on the lawn. It looked a good place to be.

'I had my own room to read and write in. We shared the cleaning and cooked our own meals. John brought his dog to see me. The staff were brilliant. I remember one day being in the lounge while they were teaching people how to set the table. I remember suddenly "coming to"; I was aware suddenly of what everyone was doing. It was like waking from a dream. *That's it*, I thought, *I'm cured*. I thought I was all set, and I left the place. I went through to Auckland. But it didn't work out. The hallucinations came back. I called John and asked him if I could return. He arranged it. He let me stay for a year, despite protests from the staff. "To give him time," he told them.

'He arranged for me to go the library every day. Over the year I read Hegel, John Stuart Mill, *Dombey & Son*, Katherine Mansfield's collected stories, James K. Baxter's collected poems and W.H. Oliver's book about Baxter. John recommended *The Screwtape Letters* by C.S. Lewis, who had tutored him at Oxford. He was writing poems himself, sonnets, I think he said. He'd written a whole sequence of them. We tried to get them after he died, but to no avail.

'After I left, he came to see me in Auckland. My mother was visiting from Australia. He picked up a cherry from a bowl on the table. "What's it like to be a cherry?" he said. He told me he said this to other doctors. "What's it like to be a cherry?" he'd say. To make them *think*. I had the feeling he was a long way ahead of them and that no one understood him.

'One of his poems was about Armageddon. "Good and evil," he said to me once. "That's what your particular illness is all about."

'We used to meet and chat, walking in the grounds. Once at a big meeting, he walked in a circle around me, almost unnoticed — to protect me from the spirits, he said. He always said there were "good dragons" at Tokanui. Then one day I heard that there were troubles. Not "trouble" exactly, but it was some sort of conflict he was facing. I asked him what it was about. He said, "Some of the Christians worship happily in the church, and the others are thrown to the lions."

'I remember seeing him off on the front lawn. He was walking down the driveway. "Ciao," he said; that was all. He waved. That was the last time I saw him. After I left the hospital, I went to Australia. Mum told me later that John had died, but she didn't tell me the circumstances. She thought it would upset me.

'I did hear from him once more, he called me in Sydney from the airport. He was flying to India, he said. He wanted to tell me something he'd been thinking about on my behalf. It lifted my spirits enormously. He had this capacity. He could be offhand and you thought he was ignoring you, yet he had this enormous empathy. I don't think there can be many others like him. He gave me my life back. It's now 25 years later and I've been teaching and directing plays and performing in Sydney and Melbourne for the past 20 years. I still feel his support.'

* * *

I have a note in one of my diaries which reads, mechanisms, not discipline. It goes back to a time when I knew John well enough to ring him up if I wanted his advice, usually about a problem in a book I was writing. One day I called him in some distress. 'Aha. A domestic?' John's voice lifted immediately.

I told him I'd begun throwing things. I had smashed Helen's favourite vase, was having some sort of breakdown. 'Oh dear,' he said.

I think the book I was writing had somehow taken over, and as far as Helen was concerned I'd become only half-human. And there was so much violence in me.

'You'd better go and see him,' Helen said.

I took the train and spent the night with John and Felicity. Next day we walked. Walked and talked. We walked through gullies and open farmland, halfway to Mount Pirongia and back. John did most of the talking. A day or so later I returned to Wellington in an altered frame of mind.

How to put it? In ancient times the old Greeks, when they suffered the anxiety of imagined curses put upon them, made sacrifices in blood or turned to seers and priests. They consulted wise men, like the singer whom Agamemnon sought out in a state of near-paralysis when his fleet was grounded at Aulis, before the battle for Troy. John had something of the singer in him. Before I left to return to Wellington, he gave me a scrap of paper which he took from his pocket. On it he had written:

MECHANISMS
not
DISCIPLINE

I have the scrap of paper still, now yellowed, pinned to my wall. I remember his words all the time, like a grace. It was a device he gave me, of course. But sometimes a device is all that we need, as John said. It is his sayings that one remembers.

* * *

Sometimes — it sounds trite, but I'll say it anyway — sometimes it's the gentle caring ones who are capable of the greatest violence. And the most successful in hiding it. John had a wild side. On a bush or mountain walk where the ways diverged, he would choose not merely the road 'not taken', in the Robert Frost sense, but the most difficult path he could find. He liked to shave the odds. When he was building his house, he insisted on digging the septic tank himself, although he had a bad back and could afford to hire a labourer. His back went into spasm and he got stuck in the hole. He had to be winched out. In his hospital work, needing to make a life-or-death decision, he would be extremely cautious, a model of responsibility and correctness. With colleagues, the reverse was often true. He once startled a gathering of psychiatrists by asserting that, mad or not, psychotic patients should observe the rules of conduct and not be 'assaultative', a view not shared by the majority in the room, who thought him unserious and probably wrote him off.

He said things that were outrageous, like all good exploratory intellectuals, usually with the aim of stimulating thought and provoking discussion. He was a provocateur. Doctors in general practice regarded him with suspicion, even our own GP in Hamilton, Anthony Rogers. Known as Rufus, he was a man of wisdom and kindliness who was so upset when he once misdiagnosed Helen's pneumonia that he visited her every day for a fortnight after she was discharged from Waikato Hospital and refused to charge a cent.

Rufus was tolerance and enlightenment personified, yet when I happened to mention the name ‘Saxby’ to him one day, he quivered and clammed up. His manner changed altogether. It was as if he could not trust himself to speak.

Enter the 1981 Springbok Tour, and Muldoon.

I had no idea of John’s involvement until he came to stay with us ten years later, when we were building the tea-house. Mention of Rufus Rogers reminds me of the event, not because of Rufus’s own stance in Hamilton, which was peripheral, on the sidelines — his surgery was smashed up by fans after he had treated protesters who had been injured — but John’s, which was planned and frontal.

John had Indian blood. It was a part of the wild animal side that was deep within him: a mysterious connection that led him on occasion to cast off restraint and expose himself to unnecessary and often extreme hardship, coupled with a complete absence of any instinct for self-preservation — as with fighter pilots. You saw it with New Zealand pilots in Malaysia and with pilots in the Battle of Britain. You see it in the following accounts of Brigadier Miles in the desert and Justice Mahon in the Erebus inquiry. As you see it with John Saxby in the days after Hamilton.

John was fond of death. It entered his conversation in unexpected ways. It entered his thoughts not in a gloomy way, but almost as a vocation, as with a parson or a priest. And it entered his verse. His poems are peopled with death besides trees and ornamental cherries. But there is another side. I wasn't aware of it until I read the poems after he died. They hint at a preoccupation with good and evil, with tyrants and dictators and men like Muldoon, and the hidden demons which were driving him and which came alive after the Tour began, possessing and pushing him almost to the brink of self-destruction.

I forget what brought the name up, probably I did. There had been a programme about the Tour on television the night before. Helen and I stayed up to watch it, but John went to bed. The next morning after breakfast, we were carrying timber and other materials up the hill to the site where the tea-house was emerging. 'John's Place', Helen called it. We paused on the lower shelf, looking out over the harbour. The sun was behind us, tipping the edge of the bay at our feet, where Hundertwasser's ketch was moored, swinging softly at anchor. It was early in the day, and the grassed shelf, like the narrow slope above where we were building at the edge of a perpendicular beech forest that encircled the bay, still moist underfoot. Muldoon's name came up in conversation. John said, 'What?' He hoisted his load, then stopped. He spoke the words 'gutter cunning'.

The words didn't surprise me; it was the way he looked. He froze. His ears went back. He became for a moment, a long moment, almost catatonic.

'You don't agree?' The man was evil, he said.

That was all. We carried on. The name didn't surface again for a couple of days, and then in a roundabout manner. We were arguing. The deck was done, the walls almost up — we were arguing about the *tokonoma*, a small alcove he wanted to incorporate in one wall so as to maintain the classical proportions. It was a Japanese tea-house, after all. I'd wanted to keep it simple. He said, 'Where's your aesthetic sense?' and stormed out on to the deck. He stood looking down on the bay. After a moment he said:

'It's still there.'

'What is?'

'His yacht. Hundertwasser's yacht.'

'It comes every summer. I think he keeps it in the Bay of Islands.'

'Hundert-wasser!' he roared. 'The man who won't draw a straight line. The name means "Hundred-Water", doesn't it? His real name was Dunkelblunt, get that.' John was a great admirer of the Austrian architect. He told me a funny story about Hundertwasser, then made up a limerick about his daughter (it rhymed with 'water'). After that, after we'd resolved the argument about the *tokonoma* and gone back to work, he began quoting limericks at random, many of his own invention, I suspect, pausing every few minutes for emphasis and waving his saw at the sky when he couldn't remember the punchline. One that I remember went:

The bishop of central Japan
Used to bugger himself with a fan.
When taxed with his acts
He said, 'It contracts—'

I interrupted him. I suddenly said, 'What d'you think Robert Muldoon would have been like if he'd grown up in Japan?'

John stopped sawing. 'Why do you say that?'

'No particular reason. I was probably thinking of the bully in him.'

'You mean the sadist in him?'

'No, the bully. He wasn't born like that. I was wondering if Japan would have made any difference.'

John picked up the saw he'd been using. He made a mark with a pencil and sat down. He said, 'Where were you in 1981?'

'In Wellington. You mean the Tour? Here in Wellington.'

'Wellington was different. It was different in the provinces.'

He said, 'People look at you as if you are mad if you say to them it may be necessary occasionally to kill someone. I spent three months in Cyprus during the EOKA emergency, shooting people and killing them in order that they didn't kill me first. In New Zealand it was more personal, less risky of course, but deeper. As far as I was concerned, it was civil war.'

He's exaggerating, I thought. We began to argue.

He said: 'You've forgotten how cleverly it was planned and orchestrated. The prime minister began by denigrating anyone who opposed the Tour by saying they were pinkos and probably perverts. Footpads and assassins. They were using the Tour as an excuse for violence on the streets. Nothing of course to do with South Africa and apartheid! It was a brilliant ploy, the sort of topic that appealed to old ladies. I can imagine Muldoon as a boy going around to old ladies and offering to mow the lawns, then nicking the plate and their underwear. And it worked! You saw it in Hamilton. What began as a small hoo-ha with the Rugby Union was escalated into a full-scale crisis by the witchery of his speeches. But it wasn't until you got to places like Hamilton, away from the capital, that you realised his speeches had the power of provocation. People were already reaching into drawers and getting their knives out.

'I spent two months telephoning rugby clubs and got nowhere. Then I thought: money. I rang up twelve people in Hamilton, and I was promised $12,000 within six hours. We mounted a campaign. I went on national TV. But it was too late; people were already entrenched. The phone calls began. "You, you fucker. We'll smash your bloody head in. Yer cunt." Et cetera.'

John's voice, normally clear and lilting, had become flat and expressionless. He was squatting on one of the joists, chin on hand. The words coming out in an unrehearsed stream.

'The calls began about midnight and went on until breakfast time. They went on for weeks. After the Hamilton game, it got worse. We had a collection of arms at the house, and sentries. Some Maori kids arrived. We didn't organise it. They came from the hospital. They simply arrived with mattresses, camped on the drawing-room floor, played cards in the evening and at nine o'clock took it in turns to go out and walk around carrying a large iron bar. Until breakfast time, when they went to bed.

'In Cyprus I was less frightened. Nicosia was fortified. We had dogs and barred gates. Here, we had an open house with nine French windows. Anyone could walk in.'

Felicity's account, when I talked to her later, was more domestic. 'After the Hamilton game, funny thing, we were unable to buy coal. Our local coal merchant plays football. "*Who* is it?" he'd say if we rang up. "Oh, Saxbys. Sorry. We've just run out." This went on for five years.'

I am quoting from notes I made at the time. Felicity had her face stove in, she said — a 14-stone Maori woman tried to break her jaw.

She said, 'Nobody dreamed we would stop the game. There were four hundred of us in the middle of the field and nine thousand baying drunken people who wanted our blood. The police said, "We cannot guarantee your safety, go off this way." We did, and the crowd in the stand erupted.'

There came a moment, John said, when he began to think of blowing up one of the coaches.

'You mean, with the Springboks inside?'

'Yes. That was the point. I'd been thinking about it for some time.'

The way to do it, he said, would be to strap on explosives and get into the bus with the South African players and himself as well. 'That way, people would simply say I was a nut and it would reflect less upon my family. So far as my children were concerned they didn't need me, they were grown-up mostly.

'But the thing became impracticable. I mean, the situation was so fluctuating. We were getting one side from the people where we lived and a completely different side from people in the city. I asked myself, will it change anything? I realised it wouldn't, even if I succeeded in blowing up the coach. I realised this sort of violent disruption would play directly into Muldoon's hands and be seen as merely proving his point. Felicity talked me out of it.'

He would have been sorry for the bus driver, John said. 'I wasn't sorry for the members of the team.'

I didn't know whether to believe him or not. Today the news of explosions and suicide bombings has become almost a daily event, in some places virtually a way of life. I remember at the time feeling shocked by what he said, as if I'd been assaulted by a blast of cyanide. But then later, after Felicity told me that in Cyprus he'd had a gun but never used it, I began to wonder. 'It was a pistol. It rusted up. He never took it out of the holster,' she said. So I wondered.

'What about Muldoon?' I said to him. 'Would you have killed him, too?'

'Certainly. If I'd had the chance.'

He went to all of the games, Felicity said, smiling now in retrospect; he'd gone on being angry and was finally satisfied only when he got to Rotorua and was arrested. I looked up the Rotorua game and met one of his companions, the MP Trevor Mallard. They had slept there on a marae, Trevor said, with half a dozen others, including a Chinese student called Hing. In the morning before it was light they had woken up the Springboks in the hotel where they were staying, causing a commotion and driving around the centre of town sounding a battery-operated foghorn machine which could be heard five kilometres away.

'We woke them up,' Trevor said, 'and made them feel they were not welcome.'

According to the police charge:

Mr Hing banged a tin and a bright object.
Mr Saxby yelled to make a noise.
Mr Mallard, the defendant in the grey jersey and glasses, stayed in the car and used the horn.

John was fingerprinted and released on bail, and told not to leave the country while the court case was pending.

Characteristically he ignored the warning and immediately flew to England.

'He scared me,' Trevor said. 'The night before when we were discussing tactics, I learned that he'd brought some incendiary devices — Molotov cocktails and petrol bombs he'd secreted somewhere and intended to use. John still believed the Tour could be stopped if there was enough disruption and violence. That's what Muldoon had said. Disruption? OK. I was happy with that. To disrupt, cause damage to property, to be arrested, I was willing for all that, but no more.'

'He wanted to go further?'

'Yes.'

'Towards violence?'

'He wanted to go further than any of us. Yes, towards violence, and including violence, if need be. That's what scared me.'

* * *

New Zealand is a country which has grave doubts about where it belongs in the world; consequently it has difficulty in defining its national character or psyche. One of the elements that helps define us, I believe, is a hidden outlaw that leads us on occasion to question authority and poke our head above the parapet. Call it dissent, subversion. Or anarchy.

> **anarchy** ***n.*** general lawlessness and disorder, esp. when thought to result from an absence or failure of government; from Latin *anarchia*, from Greek *anarkhos*, without a ruler. (*Collins Dictionary*)

It seems to surface with us in times of stress and often in wartime. I recall a couple of cases at random — James Douglas Stark and John Mulgan. James Stark—'Starkie' in Robin Hyde's *Passport to Hell* — is the brave but insubordinate outlaw in the New Zealand Expeditionary Force in the First World War; John Mulgan is the Auckland volunteer who blew the whistle on his commanding officer in the desert and had him sacked for incompetence. Mulgan is Starkie's counterpart in the Second World War. Each is part-hero, part-bandit. They are in much the same category as the Czech national hero, Schweik, in Jaroslav Hašek's *The Good Soldier Schweik*, whom the Czechs admire for his dumb insolence to the Austrian emperor and for undermining the war effort. More recently, I remember George Wilder, the North Island burglar who in the 1960s left notes of apology in the houses of his victims, tidied up afterwards and fed the cat. Wilder was actually a nasty piece of work, but he managed to stay ahead of the police for long periods on the run and became a sort of folk hero. A song of the day went:

He breaks and enters every house
To him this brings great joy
It seems his one ambition was
Policemen to annoy.

We are in a secretive way fascinated by lawlessness. It seems to be an affliction, a hidden aspect of our makeup which permeates the collective New Zealand identity, a trait yet to be explored. And not always so hidden. One of George Wilder's 'accomplices' — leaving out food and lending him a garden shed to stay in when he was on the run — was a senior academic at the University of Auckland. I am digressing, but before returning to the Charge of the Four Hundred in Hamilton, I shall continue a moment longer.

An article in the *Listener* the other day spoke of what it considered a basic trait in the New Zealand character, our conformity ('A surprising degree of conformity and resistance to change'). Before Hamilton, I would have agreed. The author of the article in the *Listener* defined New Zealanders as primarily an easy-going, stoical lot, independent, egalitarian, fair-minded. But without a whiff of the renegade in their makeup, even by implication. If you search the dictionary for a definition of 'New Zealander', you will not get one. The answer is a blank. An Austrian-American friend of ours, who is a regular visitor to this country, once wrote to me, 'I miss the serious and cheerful New Zealanders.' That's a step, you might say, in the right direction. But it's hardly a definition. An outsider might conclude that we are in some curious way indefinable. New Zealanders themselves seem unable to define themselves. We probably don't see a need. Why should we? Why bother? Our writers, with the possible exception of Bill Pearson, seem not to have noticed the subversion in our makeup. Pearson, in his essay on New Zealand behaviour, 'Fretful Sleepers', appears about to discuss this kink in our psyche — 'We have a great respect for the man who can get away with it', he says — but he then veers off into questions of puritanism and morality. His essay is brilliant and brilliantly paradoxical; it contains some withering home truths ('There is no one more docile [than the New Zealander] in the face of authority'), but it is ultimately, in its judgmentalism, disappointing.

Before Hamilton, I would have said the tendency to cock a snook at authority on a question of moral principle hardly existed here, and certainly not among the middle class. In New Zealand, doctors and psychiatrists tend to have a high profile. There is no way of knowing, but my guess is that the Saxby's stand in 1981 may have helped set a marker and produce a knock-on effect, giving the waverers and faint-at-heart a certain courage. If Hamilton tells us anything, it is that we may be a good deal less timid than we give ourselves credit for.

* * *

Two days after she was attacked, Felicity went back to work. 'Both of my eyes were black. I'd been beaten up leaving the field. I looked like a unicorn. I said to my patients, "Look, I live behind this face. I don't have to look at it all the time, but I don't want it to become a conversation. I am OK. I'm fine," I told the people in my ward at the hospital. They understood. People understood and respected me. I never knew I had a bombed face after that.

'With John, he had three days in bed. He was bruised, his thighs. He'd been twisted and jolted about trying to get onto the field — he fell and got up again and fell and got up again. His legs were quite bent.'

The Saxbys had been separated: John felled by a policeman, then thrown into the stand; Felicity was taken to hospital. Blithe, their daughter, went to find the van. It had three unconscious people in it who'd been laid out by the rugby fans.

'Our van had a big red cross on it. Every panel was kicked in and there were no windows. Then Ned [her brother] drove up. So we drove very carefully in convoy and hid the van when we got home. First we drove up to B Ward. We did it instinctively. We walked in. Some people cried. They just looked at us. Some wanted to come with us, they were afraid the house would be vandalised. There was red paint and eggs over everything when we got there. Someone came with a gun. Terry, our next-door neighbour, had been at the game. He came home and sat down with a cup of tea. He looked out and saw people bashing up our house, so he went and got his shotgun. Another guy across the road confronted them, too. Terry hung out his rugby socks on the verandah before he got the gun. He was incensed. He was a great rugby fan, but he loved us, and friendship, he obviously decided, was more important than a game of rugby. Terry's a prison officer at Waikeria.

'Some of the patients didn't hold with what we'd done, but they were upset and jolly angry. After that we never had fewer than three people living in the house or the grounds; three large men to answer the telephone and watching out for us.

'At work, people would look over their shoulder with a "Good morning, Felicity" or "Good morning, John". You didn't know if they admired you or they were glad — "Good job" kind of stuff. But gradually, as people started coming over to help, I realised how many respected us for what we'd done. It was like the Blitz in London. People would do anything for you, they rang up and said, "How are you?" "How's John?" "Are you better now?" People you hardly knew, but had stood alongside perhaps in a crowd. I was still frightened. But I didn't feel so different anymore.'

Perhaps Tokanui *was* different — an island of the bizarre in a sea of conformity. Tokanui with its panorama of villas and trees. Its complement of mental defectives. Perhaps the only place in the land where a renegade might feel protected. Sometimes it is the mad and not the multitude who are the sane amongst us.

* * *

In 1961, an adventurous young nurse, Margaret Bazley, recently arrived at Tokanui, decided to try an experiment. Margaret had begun her psychiatric training in Auckland, moved to Thames for general and obstetric training, and arrived at Tokanui as a newly fledged ward sister assigned to a wooden villa near the nurses' home. There were fifty-four women patients in the ward, from age twenty upwards: mild psychotics, schizophrenics, anorexics, 'the odd psychopath', and one involuntary resident detained under the Mental Health Act for killing her partner. Like John Saxby, who would arrive five years later, Margaret was delighted on arrival by the grounds and the park-like surrounds. She persuaded the superintendent, Dr Stallworthy, to let her run the unit as an open ward with access to the grounds and few restrictions. One of her suggestions, in an attempt to relieve the chronic under-stimulation, was to inaugurate group discussions with the patients.

'It was really more like ward meetings,' she writes, 'but it had never happened before. Not even staff meetings. A nurse would come on at the beginning of a shift, read the report from the previous shift; she knew she was the second nurse and had to count the knives and forks and put out the pig buckets. She'd just get on with it.'

Margaret recounted that at the first get-together, everyone sat around on chairs in the day room looking bemused. One of the patients was sorting clothes pegs on her lap. Margaret said, 'Would anyone like to say anything?' 'Yes,' someone said. And lapsed into silence. Margaret tried again. 'OK. Is there anything bothering anyone? Anything at all?' This time she got a response. A woman who was in the nature of keeping herself to herself and hiding in a corner, began pulling little hats from her bosom and talking about the admiral.

'She had all these hats tucked away inside her and she wanted to know if anyone had any hats for the admiral.'

Difficult not to feel for Sister Bazley and her experiment. I'm reminded of the film of Ken Kesey's book, *One Flew over the Cuckoo's Nest*, where everyone sat around in silence passively waiting for something to happen. Still, it was a start, and for Margaret Bazley 'quite a big deal to get everyone to sit in the day room and just talk about things'.

That was probably about as far as it went. Margaret had read about therapeutic communities in overseas journals, and understood at once the value of patients interacting by talking about their problems. But she left Tokanui after two years, and neither her boss, the liberal-minded Dr Stallworthy, who died suddenly of a heart attack, nor his successor, Henry Bennett, who managed to keep Tokanui out of the news for twenty years, wanted 'to sit down with a group'. When John arrived in 1966, the term 'group therapy', much less the concept, had still to enter the vocabulary.

Group therapy had begun in Europe in the nineteenth century in tuberculosis sanatoria. In Switzerland, doctors noticed how the morale of patients improved when they were encouraged to talk about their predicament. The idea caught on, crossed the channel to Britain, and by the 1960s, according to the literature, 'a revolution in social psychiatry' was under way, led by one or two enlightened hands-on psychiatrists like Maxwell Jones. At Dingleton in Scotland, we read that Dr Jones had transformed a dreary 'loony bin' into a dynamic therapeutic community. I wonder, however, if Maxwell Jones in Scotland, as John Saxby would become in New Zealand, wasn't ahead of his time.

Robert Crawford, in his book *Too Good to Last*, describes his introduction to group therapy in Edinburgh. He sat in on large group meetings of chronic schizophrenics at the Royal Edinburgh Hospital. The discussions were led, he writes, 'by a very nice senior registrar who applied the same skills to the job as if he were at a cocktail party. I was never very clear what the aim was and it was never discussed.'

Difficult to tell if such 'group discussions', shallow and meaningless, were not the rule rather than the exception in the United Kingdom.

This was the tail-end of the sixties when John had already started his experiments which would transform Tokanui's therapeutic profile. Both John Saxby and Robert Crawford were influenced by the work of Maxwell Jones. Crawford, who came to New Zealand in 1971, would put his ideas into practice at Hanmer Springs, where he created a community for drug and alcohol addicts. John visited Maxwell Jones at his hospital outside Edinburgh, Felicity's home town, and may have done a stint working with Jones. He would have observed a range of programmes for all sorts of psychiatric conditions, geared to a live-in staff and a network of links with the wider community. It's not surprising that when he came to a country which advertised its 'egalitarianism' and principles of non-discrimination, yet which shadowed and stigmatised teenagers for life because of a psychiatric history, he was in a mood to work changes.

He was quite reticent at first, even shy, according to a student nurse, Pat Forbes, who met him on the day he arrived. She describes a polite Englishman of medium height who spoke with a clipped accent. He wore a tie, blinked at the sun, and seemed both alert and reserved. If reserved, however, he was quick to learn. He got about the grounds, asked questions, seemed not to mind when strangers appeared and joined in discussions by the swimming pool.

'When he started B Ward,' a patient says, 'you never knew where the discussion might lead. "Come on," he'd say, "You lot. Get in." He'd put us in his van and we'd drive to town. He'd park in the main street and encourage us to psychoanalyse the passers-by.'

Tokanui had begun life as an overflow institution, taking the excess from several other North Island asylums, and would always to some extent get the cast-offs. Its sheer size remained a problem. There were between 500 and 600 staff handling a sprawling population of about a thousand patients, give or take, an unholy hit-and-miss atmosphere where you didn't always know who were doctors and who were patients. There were at least ten different programmes or 'hospitals' overlapping and jumbled up. This seems not to have bothered John. He sat down with an air of serious mischief and divided the hospital into three distinct parts: geriatric, disabled and psychiatric.

Soon he had opened a wing for school 'casualties'. These young patients, adolescents, mostly white, were rejects from an education system unable to handle their disorders. The unit had a daily programme of problem-solving, occupational therapy, games and activities, group discussions and visits to other wards on campus; it included a points system for home and town leave; there was a dedicated nursing and para-medical staff, from cleaner to kitchen-hand, as at Dingleton. It must have been this unit, the forerunner of B Ward, into which I stumbled when I first met John. The discussions I witnessed gave me the basis for a play, *The Mouse Man.*

B Ward. I keep mentioning it. It was housed in a two-storey red brick villa between the shop and the hospital dispensary. From its try-out for school dropouts it became a centre for group therapy; and then over the years, with the introduction of psychodrama, evolved into the first open therapeutic community in New Zealand. A Saxby statement in itself.

Psychodrama was not at first quite legitimate; that's to say, it was an object of suspicion with the hospital board. It is a treatment based on the teaching of Jacob Moreno, a Viennese psychiatrist who emigrated to America. It's designed to encourage spontaneity. Patients act out roles in a controlled situation to overcome emotional problems. Today, it is used particularly in child-abuse counselling.

Moreno had developed the concept while playing with children in the parks in Vienna and had exported it from America to Australia through Dr Max Clayton, whom John apparently met at a workshop. As did Robert Crawford of Hanmer Springs. It can take fourteen years, Crawford claims, to learn how to direct psychodrama courses. At Tokanui John didn't have that long. He had been acting out roles all his life and took to it naturally. Soon, when he became superintendent, he handed over to Felicity. The results were spectacular. Felicity, with her cut-glass English voice and oracular manner, became a star.

She said: 'John taught me. I went to dozens of workshops but he taught me. He wanted to be noticed, but he was just as happy to stay in the background. He didn't want to change the world. He wanted to make himself useful, and when he couldn't be useful anymore, he'd disappear. That's what he said.

'Psychodrama — the way it took off and helped people, including the staff, who also needed advice and support — that delighted him. He put me through it, *years* of training.

'It's all about spontaneity. How else do you encourage people who are depressed or addicted or in denial about something to change their behaviour and take responsibility for it? It's tough, I mean emotionally tough. It's not for the faint-hearted. I biffed someone once.

'You get these charged situations. It was during a workshop. A woman became offensive. She accused me of doing it for the money, and I biffed her. I knocked her to the floor. John was there. He didn't report me.'

* * *

There is a note on file in the minutes of the Waikato Hospital Board which criticises Dr Saxby, I am told, for his obnoxious behaviour. It goes on to say that on one occasion after he took over he had to be locked up. This appears to relate to the day he came on the ward and introduced himself to one and all as the new superintendent; and the equally new charge nurse, not having met him before, thought him deluded and gave him some quiet time in a padded room. If the story illustrates anything — it comes at a time of scandals in various institutions (BOY'S DEATH AT KINGSEAT ... DRUG INJECTIONS USED AS PUNISHMENT AT PORIRUA ... PATIENTS ABUSED AND HIT BY STAFF 'HEAVIES' AT CARRINGTON) — it is of lifted eyebrows and suspicion among board members at Saxby's reign of new-fangled innovations. Even the staff on campus were jittery at first.

'B Ward?' says Pat Forbes. 'It was an eye-opener. Our training hadn't fitted us for this. Some of us were terrified.'

It comes therefore as a surprise to find that, to its great credit, the board modified its stance and took courage. Faced with a rogue elephant, it decided not to banish but feed it. Workshops were held, trainers from Australia and other parts of New Zealand brought in. The hospital's in-service education centre was expanded to a 'Department'.

'Most notably,' an official report reads, 'the Department became a vibrant centre for training in new therapeutic modalities, such as psychodrama and family theatre.'

Chapeau!

The board was effectively backing a revolution in social psychiatry which in the seventies and eighties would spread throughout the country and bring psychotherapy into the institutions. Previously, psychiatric help was available only to the wealthy; ordinary people, especially women, were stuck at home with severe neuroses and nowhere to go. In Auckland, Fraser McDonald coined the term 'suburban neurosis'. It was a step in the coming feminine revolution. In Dunedin there was Roy Muir at Ashburn Hall. At Hanmer, Robert Crawford was having distinct results in the treatment of drug and alcohol addicts. I doubt if for a minute John, like his father who built a monorail for his invalid wife, thought of himself as a trailblazer.

'The fact remains,' according to Peter McGeorge who succeeded Fraser McDonald, 'that there was no college of psychiatrists in New Zealand at the time. John was working in almost total isolation. There was no one else clinically involved as he was, or who actually *thought* about these things'.

In 1984 John wrote a report on 'the aims and projects' at Tokanui. It was three pages long and appears to be about the only report he wrote that has survived. It is a model document, as lucid and precise as a sonnet. It describes the role of a hospital with 800 to 900 admissions annually to the acute areas, and the streamlining of a Victorian jumble into clinically distinct areas and wards, with programmes tailored for patients with similar needs. It describes an institution reaching out to a wider community encompassing a third of the North Island, with halfway houses and crisis intervention centres at various levels. The document is sobering. It speaks of difficulties as well as advances. It speaks of a philosophy that is visionary, but is the work of not one man but two — it masks a hidden relationship with Henry Bennett. One a Maori doctor born on a mud floor in Hastings, the other an English intellectual with an Oxford pedigree. They made an odd pair.

Tucked away on page 2 of the report was something called *Whaiora* (Wellbeing). This was a rehabilitation unit devoted entirely to Maori. We read that the unit is 'the only one of its kind in the country', as the report modestly puts it.

There wasn't much social life for the senior staff when John arrived. It revolved chiefly around dinner parties, especially those given by Superintendent Bennett and his wife, Alice, in their house amid a cluster of smaller houses near the hospital entrance. The Saxbys when they came were given the house next-door. Outwardly the two men were poles apart — one essentially an administrator tied to his desk; the other a questing hands-on clinician. Yet both were strangers to a rural backwater. John, finding his feet in a new land, was immediately captured by the fact that his boss was Maori. But Bennett himself, however secure in his Maori identity, was also finding his way as head of an institution that was predominantly Pakeha.

Bennett, the first Maori psychiatrist, was aristocracy. He was the son of a bishop. A brother, Charles, led the Maori Battalion. Another brother, John, was a top educationalist. Yet, born one of seventeen or eighteen children, Henry was nonetheless of an era and a generation where you accepted that being Maori made you one down and socially inferior. Henry Bennett was an impressive figure, tall, sartorially elegant, and experienced, and older than John by nine or ten years. He had come to Tokanui from Carrington. Before that he had been at Seacliff. In Auckland, while a senior medical officer at Carrington, he had been refused a drink at the Papakura Hotel because of his race and, unusually for one so professionally disciplined and correct, had gone public. 'If we're going to tell the world how equal Maori are in New Zealand, we're going to have to put a stop to this discrimination,' he declared. Bennett's statement made headlines, bringing him fame and notoriety. Such moments of truth, however, leave traces. The fear of a put-down is always lurking.

Bennett, meeting John for the first time, was guarded and slightly in awe of the high-flying young Pom fizzing with ideas, who, as it must have seemed, had been foisted upon him. Yet they hit it off. It was from the start a classless and equal relationship. Fuelled by wine and batting ideas across the dinner table, the newcomer learned that many of the norms he took for granted about mental health were, in a Maori context, arid. They were irrelevant. You couldn't, for example, Bennett explained, prescribe drugs to a Maori for schizophrenia.

'Why not?'

'Because in Maori medicine it doesn't exist. There's no such thing as mental illness. There are only "problems in living".'

'Say again.'

'It's a little bit different, the kind of prescription you need. We talk about the *mauri* of a person. That's different from the health of a person, and it's different from not having an illness. Think of it this way: Maori health is whanau-based.'

'*Whanau?*'

'Family. It's a tribal thing. If you say to a Maori, "How are you?", you won't get an answer probably. Why not? Because you're not family. A man who's just tried to gas himself or hang himself will give you a big grin, as if there's nothing wrong. You have to go in a great big semi-circle if you want to get at what the problem is.'

'Like in Africa.'

'No, John, not like in Africa. I've never been to Africa. Like in Polynesia.'

'*Fascinating*,' John said. 'I'll have to think about it.'

That conversation — I'd like to say it's based on anecdote, however it isn't. It's invented. It is entirely imaginary. But you get the idea.

John's moment of truth came when it dawned on him — or was brought home to him by a Scottish psychiatrist and colleague at Tokanui, Flora Rose, who was a frequent and convivial dinner guest — that he had landed slap in a part of the country where Maori outnumbered Pakeha roughly two to one. *And yet*, as she said, 'And yet we never see any Maoris in the hospital, hardly any. Why is that?'

She sounded bemused, but it got John thinking. *Gobsmacked*, he admitted later. He began asking Bennett questions: *Shouldn't something be done?*

Curiously, Bennett was resistant. The demographics of Maori versus Pakeha were not, after all, his main concern. Nevertheless, John's questioning did not stop there — a conversation had begun. It was a conversation, such was Bennett's reluctance to favour Maori in an almost exclusively white hospital environment, that would continue for nearly twenty years before anything happened. Matters began to change only in the mid-seventies. Increased urbanisation, the emptying of maraes, the alienation of Maori from their roots, meant that Tokanui at a certain point was targeted. It became a refugee centre for scores of young Maori misfits and social rejects, who were adrift in the towns and cities and cast out. Many could not read or write. Only then it seems did Henry Bennett sit up and take notice. What I am writing here is grossly brief and simplistic; it ignores the involvement of young Maori health professionals and many others with links to community organisations in the cities who were already banging on John's door urging him to act.

A witness to this is Geraldine Keith, a family friend and familiar and intimate of both households. She served several stints at Tokanui before setting up her own practice as a clinical psychologist.

She says: 'Most of these conversations began at the swimming pool or around the table. John, when he got his teeth into something, didn't let go. He was insatiably curious, and it was his persistent questioning I believe that enabled Henry [Bennett] to begin crystallising things in his mind, and in the end accept that John was right.'

Even so, a long conversation getting longer, and it wouldn't be until Bennett retired that a specific Maori health unit would be up and running.

Whaiora had eighteen beds and few rules; it encouraged the patient on being discharged to be 'a better person' — for himself and for others to live with. Those were 'the aims'. The report gave no further details. The unit was a success. *Whaiora* transcended race. It encapsulated in its openness an entire philosophy that made Tokanui what it was, and it was copied by other institutions up and down the country. *Whaiora* would remain in being for some years after John's death, a testimony and a testament. Yet without Bennett's resistance to help fuel the Saxby energy, it might never have happened — another way of saying that *Whaiora* represented, in Geraldine's view, 'yet another connection across the mysterious Indian part of his identity that enabled John to come to terms with a new land'.

* * *

I have to keep reminding myself that this is not a biography of John Richard Baber Saxby, any more than it is a history of Tokanui Hospital. It is at most a sketch, a patchwork attempt to illuminate the enigma of a man who travelled with little luggage, who changed lives and touched hundreds, who advertised his intention to depart the planet in letters ten feet high, yet who, when he carried out this intention and took his life as planned, caught everyone with the exception of his wife entirely by surprise.

Many were angry at the way he died. They are still angry today. It is perhaps a measure of his quality that many people were so angry that they couldn't bear to come to the house for his funeral service.

John spoke of his intention to commit suicide not just to close friends and colleagues. He spoke of the genetics of depression and its application to completed suicides; he foretold the method which in his own case might be best. 'Yes,' he said matter-of-factly to a staff nurse, Judy Beasley, when called to a hanging, 'that's the way I'd like to go.' Drug overdose, he considered unreliable. He spoke of bushcraft and survival. Out walking with a woman friend in the Coromandel, hiking through the bracken, he showed her an instrument he carried, to use if he ever found himself in a corner or got 'into difficulties'. He spoke of suicide, Felicity said, 'as he spoke of putting out the milk'. To Helen and me there were only hints. But they were, Lord knows, strong enough.

My mind goes back yet again to the time he came to Wellington when, as it seems in retrospect, we talked nonstop for three weeks. Each morning we climbed the seventy-odd steps to the hillside where we were building the tea-house, as he insisted on calling it. John bounded up. Older than I at 63, fit and nimble on his pins (easy to see why he became a para), he always reached the top first. As a teenager he had hitchhiked to the Lake District to climb. His daughter Halcyon showed me a photograph of him dangling in space in Snowdonia; on the back he had written in Latin, *A riddle inside a conundrum.* He had once contemplated, she said, 'doing a Chris Brasher' by attempting to climb the twenty-two peaks in Wales in the course of a single day.

At Lowry Bay, on reaching the top, he would fall down gasping for breath, then stand up groaning and holding his back. He groaned like a dying walrus. It was a pose. We'd both laugh. Occasionally he'd say, if he dropped something on his foot, 'Why do things keep going *wrong*?' One morning he started hammering where he'd left off the day before, then stopped. He said: 'The only pleasures to look forward to in this life are bad things stopping happening.' He smiled, and went on hammering.

I don't know if the changes at Tokanui that would dismantle most of his work at a stroke had begun or not, but I didn't take what he said literally. I thought no more about it until a year or so later when we spent some days together on the west coast and he said it again in another way. We had slept the previous evening at his house, where I remember a hospital colleague arrived after dinner. He was in a state. He and John stayed up talking late. I asked him about it the next morning, or Helen did. He said, 'Yes, the elephants were at it again.'

Elephants?

'Oh,' he said. 'Yes, they're everywhere.' He added evasively: 'Until I came, they were almost unknown.'

This was next day. We had driven to Kawhia on the west coast and were sailing down-harbour in the milk launch to the remote headland of Te Maika, where Helen and I lived for many years. For us, it was a kind of pilgrimage and nostalgic return after nearly ten years. For John and Felicity it was a first sight of the North Island's west coast. John had a patrician head, wide-set blue eyes, a strong jaw and a brow furrowed with evenly drawn lines like the runnels in a ploughed field.

'*Elephants?*' I repeated.

But he wouldn't be drawn. He often spoke elliptically, and when he did he had a tic, a habit I've noticed among people who whistle or cough when they're about to tell a lie — his ears pointed. As they did now. He turned the question, saying, 'I stole the expression from Nehru. It was Jawaharlal Nehru who said it first. "Japan," he said, "has many reasons to be sad, and elephants are almost unknown there." I think it comes from Nehru.'

His ears pointed again and he smiled, looking out towards the promontory that was our former home. The light was on the grasses on the sandhills, glowing amber and gold along the foreshore. By then he must have been, at least partly, in denial.

Yet it was a good visit. John, the man who wanted to know everything, was curious from the moment we landed. 'What's it like? Coming back here again? It must be like becoming married again to the same woman. I can't imagine it.'

We climbed the black hills, combed the reefs and shoals and walked the beaches; we collected mussels, and in the evenings smoked fish over an antediluvian barbecue I had made years earlier, which the new owner, Phillip Green, bless him, had preserved. The wind blew, the light a constant renewal. In the evening the light over the Tasman Sea towards Raglan was amber. We sat outside, listening to the wheedle of the McWhirter birds above the low rumble of surf. Beyond the surf-line, Mount Karioi rose stark on a band of purest apricot.

John said, 'It's real New Zealand. You have the feeling that the day before you, longer than any other, holds a promise greater than any other.'

It was probably one of the last good times. Later, when we got home, we received a letter of thanks which spoke of his coming to Wellington again.

It mentioned the hospital and the redundancies and, for the first time, that weasel word 'restructuring'. But he sounded confident. There was 'a ray of hope'. We must have known in a vague way that something was going on, yet were not alarmed. We left for Berlin soon afterwards. The Te Maika visit remains etched in my mind.

From my diary:

Monday Jan 21st
John fell in, carrying Rosie [his dog], on the way to the mussel reef. 'It's so warm!' he yelled. Evening, we all cooked, then played word games. 'How about,' he said, 'we set up a Society for the Restoration of Lost English Positives? "Gruntled", for example.

'Ept,' *he added.*

'Rascible,' *Helen suggested.*

And Felicity, 'Couth.'

Me, 'Embowelled.'

John, laughing: 'Yes, yes. As in, "I am embowelled *and getting better all the time".'*

* * *

We laughed a great deal. The visit lasted four days. I assumed he had simply taken time off, that he was still in charge. We took the launch back to Kawhia and drove home to Wellington, stopping with them again overnight. We sat up talking and reminiscing. In the morning we found John in his dressing gown rummaging about in his collection of LP records. He found what he was looking for — it was the Amadeus recording of Schubert's C Major Quintet — and gave it to Helen. ('Jim says you love this recording.') As we were leaving, he came out to the car and put a book inscribed for Jim from John in my hand.

'You might find it interesting,' he said.

It was a book set in Greece by a writer I'd not heard of, Kay Cicellis, and entitled *Death of a Town*. I read the book and found it both curious and interesting, but no more than that. Only now, looking back, do I see it for the metaphor he must have intended.

Death of a Town is about the lives of some people caught up in an earthquake in Greece. It begins with the words: 'I am looking at a picture. It is framed: four straight lines enclose it: one can concentrate: one knows exactly what one is looking at.'

If I look at a picture of Tokanui Hospital as it must have been when John arrived from England, I can see in my mind's eye a town of small villas and bungalows set among trees and gardens, and, out of sight at the top, bleeding off the edge of the picture, a farm of some 1200 acres where the residents worked, with its own farm manager, its ploughman and its carpenter. Population, including staff, between one and two thousand. The gardens are immaculate. Some of the residents are working in the gardens, others in the orchards, others are cutting fresh flowers and collecting fruit to supply the houses, still others are simply wandering about or being put into a trailer contraption to be taken to the swimming pool where over the course of time, according to the chaplain, or parson as he was known, three-quarters of the long-term and able-bodied residents have learned to swim. There is a library, a recreation hall, a woodwork shop, a bakery, a laundry, a small school on the edge of what appears to be a sports ground, a cricket field, and several bigger buildings serving a variety of purposes, including a nurses' home and nursing training centre and a chapel with its own chaplain.

'*Welcome* [says the smile on the face of the chaplain], *if you have a sense of God. If not, a sense of humour will do.*'

I am sentimentalising the picture, but not over-much, I hope. The residents are different from us but not entirely different; they dress as we do and don't wear red or yellow stars on their clothing; the main difference is that many of them have been here a long time and aren't going anywhere. How many? You'd be surprised. In the beginning most of them stayed put, the chronics and permanents. Now, with the new therapies and a halfway house in Hamilton to help jump-start the younger ones back into the community, the situation is reversed. Some of the residents move on. How many? To be honest, about two-thirds of them. Their stay at Tokanui is quite short. It's what is called a healthy turnover.

In 1967, the farm was closed. Still, it was happening at other rural asylums, too. It wasn't a death blow. There was one other loss, the chapel. The chapel burned down and was not replaced. For the next twenty years, until 1987 when a new Mental Health Act was passed, all was well. The Act occurred during the Labour/Roger Douglas monetarist years, remembered by some as the dawn of a new day (Hail to Thee, dear Cost-cutters!) and by others as a deadly virus (there was a fever in the rate of suicides). The Act was succeeded the following year by a damning government report, known as the Mason Report, after a series of alleged scandals at other institutions. The Act determined, in the language of the day, 'a more managerial approach'. Such terminology, indicating the subjugation of the human and the caring to political and medical arrogance, was new to this country. At Tokanui it would result in the destruction of everything vital and spontaneous, although this was not immediately apparent. One of the first to encounter it was a young staff nurse, Jill Harris.

Jill emerged from her ward one morning after breakfast to find two strangers in suits on the doorstep. They were male, middle-aged and seemed friendly. They introduced themselves. One said to Jill, immaculate in her white nurse's cap and starched tunic (you don't see them like that anymore): 'Those women over there, what are they doing?'

'They're weeding in the garden. You can see.'

'And those blokes with ladders? Where are they going?'

'Probably to the orchards. Why don't you ask them?'

'How much do you pay them?'

'Pay? Don't be silly. They live here, it's their home.'

'So you don't pay them anything?'

'I've told you.'

'It's not right. It's slave labour.'

Jill laughed. She said, 'I don't think you understand what this place is all about.'

'It's slave labour, I reckon. We're going to change that.'

The visitors moved on. She says that she thought, in her bemused state, that they were a couple of do-gooders.

* * *

One of the first to notice that John was under strain was the Scots psychiatrist, Dr Crawford, at Hanmer Springs. Robert Crawford was involved in the treatment of drug and alcohol addiction. The two men had something in common: each had broken new ground in techniques of clinical training and the handling of previously unmanageable cases. Hanmer, especially, was having visible results in the alleviation of drug addiction. They had arrived from the United Kingdom at about the same time, had met at conferences and workshops in New Zealand and at Perth in Australia, and had come to respect and admire each other's work, especially in the use of psychodrama.

They discussed the Mason Report and the new Act. The former spoke of 'serious deficiencies' in the system. The Act created a new post of Director of Psychiatric Services, and contained the news that an asylum didn't necessarily need to be run by a psychiatrist or even a doctor. It could be simply 'a manager'. Terrific, John said. Crawford agreed. He spelled it out.

'It's the Toyota Way. Anyone on the shop floor can become a manager. A cleaner can become a neurosurgeon.' Robert Crawford had recently been at a medical conference which had savaged the Act. Speakers pointed out that, while the Toyota Way might be good for producing motor engines, it didn't do much for human ones, which relied on love and trust and had a certain moral and ethical dimension. I think Robert Crawford took an even dimmer view of the Act than his guest did.

'John stayed with us. He came for the weekend. Hanmer, as you know, is quite elevated: the spa backs onto mountains and has some rough terrain leading to the alps, quite perilous. Easy to get lost. In the morning John went off. He didn't say where he was going. He was poorly equipped, didn't have the right clothes, nothing to eat. He just walked into the mountains with a handful of oatmeal in his pocket. He was gone all day. He came back eventually, sometime in the night, but I was worried. He was my responsibility. I was worried sick.'

It was a sign, one of the signs. After he resigned, we have only signs to go on.

He resigned as medical superintendent in the wake of the Mason Report, when a decision, as it seems, had already been taken behind closed doors to close Tokanui.

In an interview published after his resignation, John was regretful, but he also expressed hope: the important services and mechanisms that had been put in place would survive, he predicted. Indeed at this stage almost everything was still functioning.

'People would travel huge distances from around the country to attend Felicity's sessions,' says a colleague. 'She was the draw. Psychodrama was her passion. She had the ability to put light into people's eyes. She stayed to the end. We all knew it would never be the same again.'

In 1989, Tokanui's full-time music therapist, the only one in the country, was discharged, followed by about eighty other staff. It was done quietly. Possibly the cost of what would follow — the emptying of the swimming pool, the closing of the recreation hall, activities, games, movies, workshops, the disappearance of the colour green, the abolition of the nursing school and the training centre, the removal to a concrete facility in the city hemmed in by an urban environment — would not have been so awful had the uplifting of the goods and chattels, the patients, not been so arbitrary and drawn out. The process would drag on for years. 'Save Tokanui Hospital' petitioners would still be banging on the doors of Parliament in Wellington six years later.

And yet (said the men in suits), why the surprise? Tokanui had been 'the Cinderella' of the system for far too long. Had 'had its day'. Was no longer 'appropriate'. Perhaps the men in suits were right. The trend in favour of accommodation 'in the community' was now world-wide, however inadequate the accommodation might be.

Don't let's forget the irony. It concerns John's predecessor and admirer, Henry Bennett, the man who had demolished the fences and ushered in 'the open hospital'. It was Henry Bennett who had developed innovations like music therapy. This is the same Henry Bennett who had helped to write the Mason Report, the document more than any other that sounded the death-knell for Tokanui.

In his interview, giving the reasons for his resignation, John doesn't mention the fact that the hospital's days are numbered. He's probably not aware of it yet. What he says is that he has decided to withdraw from a system which is futile. He's sick of constantly having to fight the mandarins of the Justice Department over questions like the committal of so-called 'dangerous' patients. Whose responsibility was *that*?

At the end of the interview, he said: 'I was worn down, by personal denigration and decided that it might be justified.'

Another sign?

* * *

A middle-aged doctor in trouble has very few places to turn. We know this from a variety of sources and studies. He expects others to come to him, but he himself, when in trouble, will avoid seeking the very aid that will ease his pain. One person who saw the lights changing was Maros Hollóköi, the young Hungarian psychiatrist who arrived when the dismantling was just beginning. About this time Felicity wrote to us when we were in Berlin, saying that John was on a slag heap, as she put it. 'He's been relegated to the front wards and shortly he's going to be sent out in a car to do the outpatient clinics.'

Maros arrived in 1990. He and John worked together, joked, ate together, went to the pub in Kihikihi together. They hiked up Mount Pirongia together ('He walked so fast, I thought he'd have a heart attack'), they saw each other every week. They did the clinics together.

'There were a number of outpatient clinics — Tokoroa, Mangakino, Te Kuiti, Taumarunui, Putaruru. We drove about not in his terrible little car, but in a hospital car. Thanks be. He talked all the way. He loved the countryside, the autumn leaves, the changing hills. "God's sakes," he'd say, if he was tense or angry. That's the only thing I noticed, he was driving too fast. "God's sakes, John," I'd say. "Take care. *Please.*" I'd been a pilot. Before I left Budapest, I was training to be a fighter pilot. I was used to speed. But the way he drove sometimes, he frightened me.'

Now the chronology and sequence of events starts to get confusing. According to Maros, the year after John resigned as superintendent he was made redundant. Rendered 'surplus to requirements', he was forcibly retired. But this can't be right, since Felicity says he had gone on working part-time, as a consultant. 'He couldn't bear to stay away,' she said.

At some point we must have had an inkling of the 'restructuring' going on. Helen says she once asked him about it. 'He didn't seem upset. It was still a place worth working in. He even defended some of the changes taking place. He laughed. "Oh well," he said. "If it comes to the worst, we can always live on rice."'

Suicide is one of the last great moral and philosophical questions, we are told, in that it is about the value of life itself. The sense of it, if sense there be. Death is something John talks about a lot in his poems, when he isn't talking about roses. (He always put a fresh rose in Helen's room when she stayed.) Sometimes he is serious, sometimes philosophical. In a poem written in 1988, called 'Trip', he views death as a gesture or a new dance step he's learning but hasn't quite mastered.

I think by the time he decided to kill himself he had brooded so endlessly on the details, that death itself had become almost a sideshow. In his famous study, *The Savage God*, Al Alvarez says that to the outsider suicide may seem a motiveless perversity. Alvarez quotes the writer Cesare Pavese, who killed himself at forty-two at the height of his creative powers and his worldly success. I think in John's case, however, Camus is more relevant. Camus says a suicide is born, not made. Afterwards, we, the ones left behind, we wonder. We go on wondering. We are assailed by feelings of guilt. We look for reasons. *Why?* We want to know. The reasons that are usually given — humiliation, rejection, failure in love, injured self-esteem, extreme sickness — may be absolutely authentic. But they say nothing at all about the slow sapping of spirit, the secret inner torture and hidden processes which lead up to it.

'An act like this,' Camus said, 'is prepared within the silence of the heart, as is a great work of art.'

One of John's poems is a sonnet called 'Dispatch'. It begins:

On or about the third Saturday
Of March, of the year 2000
At 3 o'clock in the afternoon
(And in a small gathering of friends),
I shall take possession of the rest

Of my life ...

'Dispatch' was written in 1989, the year before he visited Te Maika. The timing in the second line, 'March, of the year 2000', seems a long way out. It's the sort of clue planted to mislead the reader you would expect in a novel by Agatha Christie. He had about four years to live.

* * *

He did a strange thing. He went to Kashmir. I received a letter posted on my birthday. I have the envelope still. (The letter is lost and I no longer remember the contents.) The letter was written, if I read the date-stamp correctly, from 'PAHALGAM Kashmir'. A couple of months later (he must have gone back), I had another postcard from the same place.

'Where have you *been*?' I said, the next time we met.

'Oh, I stayed with some people, farmers. Lovely family. In a little village. I did some climbing. Had a lovely time.'

There was a legend in the family, he said — meaning his family — that they came from Kashmir. John was christened John Richard Baber Saxby, his father was Oliver Baber Saxby, John's son, 'Ned', was Felix Edward Baber. And he'd had gone to India to find out about it, if it was true.

And is it?

Absolutely, he replied.

(He said the link was with Tamerlane the Great. One of Tamerlane's descendants, Sultan Baber, had plundered Kashmir in the sixteenth century. Baber was one of John's forebears.)

'But you went *twice*.'

'Yes. It was an exciting time.'

The first time, he said, General Zia-ul-Haq was assassinated. His plane exploded with the general in it on the night John arrived. As he was leaving, a bridge was blown up behind him. He returned the next day to find the village where he was staying razed to the ground.

The second time he went, a civil war was in progress. That must have been the tail-end of 1991. The next thing I remember is a flurry of postcards and a letter dated November 1992 from England, written by Felicity.

'John has acquired a campervan for our travels,' she wrote, sounding in high spirits. He had been in Oxford to sell the house in Abingdon, both his parents having died, and afterwards had taken a hospital job, apparently a mistake. The work was drudgery. Now they were off for a holiday, intending to travel in France and picnic in the van for meals. But that hadn't gone to plan either.

'Rained out,' he wrote in a postcard. 'Finally defeated by rain ...'

They came back, to what I don't know. We heard nothing. The silence was relieved when Helen's car broke down. She was driving back after visiting her parents in Hamilton; John rescued her and insisted she spend the night. Downstairs where she slept, she found he'd been insulating the lower rooms with polystyrene. One of the windows was boarded up. It struck her as odd. But the next morning they'd had an animated discussion about some plans he had drawn up to reorganise our house in Wellington.

'He's made lots of drawings,' she said to me. 'He promised to come down again.'

We received a strange phone call one night. It was a winter's evening, July or August. We had come in from eating out in town. Helen answered the phone. I was downstairs. She called out: 'It's John. He wants to ask you something.'

'He's ringing from the hospital,' she said when I came up. I heard her say, 'On duty? You mean you're still *there*?' 'He's gone back,' she said, covering the mouthpiece. 'He hasn't retired.' Then I heard her say, with a little yelp of delight, '*When are you coming?*' There'd been an exchange of letters about our house, an ongoing discussion with Helen about enlarging it so that we could take visitors. But no, he said, he couldn't come. He was rather busy. That wasn't the reason for his call.

She said, 'He wants to ask you something. A favour, I think.' She handed me the phone. Oh nothing in particular, he said. He was 'writing something' but couldn't make up his mind. That was all. He talked about Rosie, their dog. Rosie had died. We chatted on. He asked what I was writing, and said that Ned, their son, was coming to stay. He asked to speak to Helen again, and told her what a disaster their trip to Europe had been. But we knew that already from his postcards. He chatted away inconsequentially, and rang off.

Helen said, 'What was that all about?' 'No idea,' I said. She said, 'What was the favour he wanted?' 'He didn't say.'

We were both puzzled. It was only later, after Felicity rang, that we worked it out, the reason for his call. He had rung to say goodbye.

He had been at the hospital all day, seeing patients and writing up notes, and had continued working late into the evening. Felicity was not home that day. He was using an old office in Ward 21 that had once been her office and was now mainly used as an interview room, past the day room as you entered the ward by a corridor. Ward 21 was a rehab ward. The day room was a cheerful place opposite the dining room — the patients' rooms were further down, off the corridor — with coloured posters and children's drawings on the walls, and a table-tennis table.

He had come on duty and made the rounds in the morning, much as usual. He returned a book to a patient with a note, thanking the lender. At 10.30 he attended a meeting. Jenny Rankin, a colleague, says that an hour later he rang to remind her about a wire to protect a tree that he'd planted for her as a house-warming present. She was a new neighbour. He made several phone calls and left notes for various people in the course of the day. One call was to the garage about his car. It needed a new seat belt. It wasn't ready. 'Well, get it ready,' he said. '*Now.*' He was short-tempered, Judy Beasley, the charge nurse recalled. But he was often short-tempered after lunch. I am piecing this together in fragments from what staffers told me. It seems important to tell it, however fragmentary, because it was important to *them*. I had the very strong sense that, despite his waywardness and occasional bad temper, if anything was to be written about that day in September 1993, they wanted to be there, too, as if by right: as if he belonged to them and not the bureaucrats who'd shafted him; nobody else had energised or empowered them to believe they had it in them to realise their full potential.

'Two things he said to me I'll never forget,' said Tony Moran. '*Tony, you're never wrong.*' And: '*Yes. We should think about that.*'

He cancelled one appointment, Judy said, and rang his wife. In the afternoon he spent nearly an hour with a former patient whose mother had died 'of depression'. He explained to the patient that depression didn't cause paralysis or death, but might be linked to the mother's Parkinson's — 'Even if,' as he said afterwards in a note left for Felicity, 'the treating physician was unwilling to admit it, and defeat!'

'I was very busy today and didn't get round to ringing about the yellow car,' he said in another note.

Angela van Gogh, the afternoon nurse, found him writing at his desk. He left the desk clean and tidy, 'as he always did'. He was still working late in the night. She remembers him coming in wearing his fawn suit and carrying a manila folder under his arm. He arrived at about ten to eleven. 'He looked awful, as if he'd been crying. He seemed to have lost track of time. "What's the time?" he said. I said, "John, it's late," and shooed him off home. But he went back to the office. The folder was sticking out underneath his jersey.' One of the old hands, Bob Elliott, reminded him he had an appointment at eleven the next morning. He said, 'I might be a little late.' That was strange, Angela thought. 'John was never late.' Later still a car drew up outside. 'He said, "Who's that?" I told him it was the next shift coming on. He said, "Is it that late?"'

Angela came off duty at 11.30pm. As she drove past the house in Te Mawhai Road she had a premonition and stopped the car. She noticed a light on downstairs. She drove on. Felicity was away, attending a psychodrama conference in Hamilton. She came home in the afternoon the next day, Thursday, to find him dead in one of the bedrooms downstairs.

DISPATCH

On or about the third Saturday
Of March, of the year 2000
At 3 o'clock in the afternoon
(And in a small gathering of friends),
I shall take possession of the rest

Of my life, which no doubt latterly
Will have become far more burden
Even than it's proved up till now
Reckoning that what it presents
Constitutes my own profit or loss

Upon a freely-made investment —
And to be disposed as I see fit
Thus my last will and testament
Will be that I do so as of right.

December 1989

TRIP

The world is very beautiful — I've seen it;
But when it is no longer seen by me
I doubt if the philosophers will deem it
To suffer any major injury,
Or fear for its continuing to be.

And there's another thing: I would expect it
To alter only trivially with time,
Remaining largely as I recollect it
For several generations after mine
I shan't miss out on very much by dying.

So cheerio the world and what is in it —
I have already seen enough for me;
I think it warrants a hasty visit,
But I'm away to taste eternity.

1988

‘Trip’ was written for his friend, Maros Hollókoï, and was read by Maros to the congregation gathered for John’s funeral service. Neither ‘congregation’ nor ‘service’ are the right words. ‘Wake’ does not convey the sense of it either. I don’t know how many people came to the house to pay homage on that day. They were there in droves — in the big room upstairs where he lay by the window, in the nook as you came in at the door, on the stoop beneath the silk tree and the ramp like a bridge leading down from the front entrance; they stood on the steps and gathered on the lawn and in the driveway past the magnolia tree as far down as the wintersweet he had planted by the main road, still flowering after winter and giving off its lemony scent. It was a Monday, the last Monday in September. He hanged himself on Wednesday or the Thursday, sometime after midnight. It was not known exactly when.

Felicity rang us in Wellington with the news. He had finished, she said. ‘There’s nothing more to say, is there?’

‘Please come,’ she said.

Helen was distraught, but was unable to leave Wellington. I felt numbed. I could hear a bell ringing, faintly, in the distance, that I had heard ring before.

I drove up with Geraldine Keith, who had been there at the start of things. She had come to Tokanui originally at the instigation of Henry Bennett, who had studied medicine with her father in Dunedin. 'He taught me everything,' she said, meaning John. 'He taught me to think.' She said it again, addressing the gathering the following morning. Henry Bennett, whom I had not known was still alive, was one of the last to speak. He addressed the coffin directly: 'Farewell, my friend. You have always been in control, and you are still in control. No reira, tena koe, tena koe. My friend John.'

The tributes went on all morning.

He lay in an open coffin, looking across the fields to Mount Pirongia. That morning when we awoke, there was dew on the grass, the slopes of the mountain banded by mist. Felicity said, when the coffin arrived, 'We'll put him by the west window.' I thought, of course. It was his place. He lay on a low couch, covered by a quilt, his face in repose, benign, beautiful. At first people entering the room seemed reluctant to approach; others stood outside in the spring chill, seemingly diminished as if excluded or somehow cheated by an event for which they were unprepared. Then a delegation of Maori arrived intoning a *karakia*. They flung a cloak over the body. The sound of their incantation filled the morning and a change occurred. I had witnessed a similar change once before.

At Jerusalem on the Whanganui River a group of Pakeha writers and poets who had assumed an entitlement and prepared tributes for the funeral of James K. Baxter, were swept aside by local Maori whose grief transformed the event into something else entirely. With John, it was less dramatic, but the change was equally marked. People began coming forward. They shed their inhibitions. You could tell from their body language as they approached and bent over the coffin. They began to talk to him. They reached out and they touched him, and a kind of serenity seemed to settle.

It was something you thought about only afterwards, and was symbolised I believe by the cloak, which was a *korowai* cloak, thickly woven and crossed in many colours. It had belonged to a Maniapoto chieftain. The new arrivals wrapped the cloak around him in their *aroha*.

He had become in their eyes a *rangatira*.

Later in the day he was taken to the hospital and lay in state. It was as if a switch had been thrown. People in one ward who had been sitting around or dozing uttered little cries and came forward and touched him. Late in the afternoon he was taken to *Whaiora*, the Maori unit, where he lay downstairs in the foyer, surrounded. My memory of the afternoon has dulled, except for an incident that occurred the next day when I returned to *Whaiora* with Geraldine to take photographs. A young man, warrior type, materialised from nowhere and presented her with a flower. I had noticed him the previous afternoon when the coffin was brought in. One of his jeans was agape, torn at the knee. During the tributes he stood aside, tearing at the threads. At the end he came forward and stood by the coffin, fingering the cape covering John's body, a strange febrile eagerness of expression on his face. He paused and crossed himself. He made as if to speak. Suddenly, looking down, he threw wide his arms. The gesture said it all.

* * *

I read a book many years ago called *A Fortunate Man.* It is about a country doctor named Sassall and his commitment to his patients in a village in the Forest of Dean. To widen his experience he makes a kind of Faustian bargain with his patients, and is rewarded by being absorbed into their families, and granted the intimacies of a father-friend. But there is a price. He suffers the cost of unbearable pressure, and also from a sense of his own inadequacy. Depression sets in and in the end he is consumed.

Dr Sassall left England and went to China, where his death, in 1982, deepened the enigma of his life. John, dying eleven years later, might be almost an older brother.

'He was finished,' Felicity said to me. 'He was worn out. I'd had only fourteen years at it. He'd had forty.'

Theirs is a universal story. The doctor cures others to cure himself. In John there was great sensibility and tenderness. He had a natural, almost preternatural understanding for those in trouble, but in the end his openness to experience and to his patients' needs — his gift — was his undoing.

He had once told us he was translating Rilke from the German. We'd always known about his interest in poetry, but until his phone call, telling us he was writing something, we had no idea he was actually producing it. He wrote altogether ninety-seven unpublished sonnets.

They were bundled up in a padded envelope and left for Felicity to find. They were neatly typed, together with the holograph originals written in ink in his clear, flowing hand, and contained inside a loose UNICEF diary folder. Felicity showed them to me. 'There's a note,' she said. 'He wants to ask you a favour.' I read the note, and I remembered his mysterious phone call — Helen handing me the receiver, saying: '*He wants to ask you a favour.*' And then, when I'd hung up:

'What was it?'

'He didn't say.'

And now he did. I read the note Felicity gave me. It was about the sonnets. Would I write to Brigid Brophy for him and ask her advice, with a view to possible publication? Brigid Brophy had been John's friend and contemporary at Oxford in the 1940s; she had become a novelist and leading figure in the England of the 1960s 'permissive society'. She was still a name in British letters. I duly wrote, as John asked. But Brigid Brophy was then ill. Her husband replied, saying that she was nearing the end of a long battle with multiple sclerosis.

'I have in part,' she wrote of the disease which had trapped her inside the house, 'died before the event.' It comes to me now that exactly the same might be said of John, at the time of his phone call.

REGINALD MILES

One morning in the winter of 1911 a shy youth with piercing blue eyes left his native New Zealand to embark on a course of higher studies in Australia. From his appearance and reticent manner you would not have guessed that the college he was about to enrol in was a military one; or that three years later he would graduate with top honours at the head of its first intake; or that thirty years after that, now a brigadier with a David Niven moustache, he would be recommended to take command of the New Zealand Division, then fighting in the Mediterranean in the closing stages of the Second World War. His name was Reginald Miles. Reggie for short, or Reg. He was seventeen years old when he left New Zealand, and his transformation from tentative schoolboy to top cadet, the proud possessor of 'Graduation Certificate No. 1' at the Australian Royal Military College Duntroon, confirmed his father's worst fears. As the saying goes, 'When a soldier is born into a family, the family is finished.'

Miles was first tipped to lead the Division by the prime minister, Peter Fraser. This was in 1941. The Second World War was eighteen months old. Miles was in Egypt rebuilding his dismembered Artillery, having led it through the fatal campaign in Greece. Two years later, in 1943, he was again first choice to take over the Division, proposed this time by the commander General Freyberg himself, despite the fact that when last seen together the two men were barely on speaking terms, and that at the time Miles was unable to report for duty, having been captured in the desert and locked up in a fort in the north of Italy.

Nevertheless, on 10 May 1943, Freyberg, fighting with the Division in southern Italy and anticipating his own elevation to command a corps, wrote to the government in New Zealand and recommended Miles as probably the man best-qualified for the job — 'if available'. The moment had seemed propitious.

But unknown to Freyberg or almost anyone else, five weeks earlier Miles had made a daring escape from Italy and was now trapped more securely than ever in neutral Switzerland. With him was another New Zealand brigadier, James Hargest. The pair had tunnelled their way underneath a fortress outside Florence, thereby becoming the two highest-ranking Allied officers ever to escape from captivity in two world wars. Miles, burning to rejoin the New Zealanders in the south, was the more senior man.

'We want him back,' reads a memorandum by Freyberg.

Poor Miles. It was proving easier to get into Switzerland than out. He was desolate. In the weeks and months to come, Freyberg and Fraser would be equally frustrated. It was no cakewalk to smuggle a general in wartime out of Switzerland and on to England, even with the help of MI9 and the French underground. The director of military intelligence in London informed the New Zealand prime minister that, since the Germans had occupied the south of France, 'the position with Switzerland has become extremely difficult'.

Eventually, however, a way would be found.

With the aid of the Dutch and French resistance networks, Miles, disguised as a peasant, would be ferried to safety — smuggled across occupied France, over the Pyrénées and into Spain. He would cross the border into northern Spain in high spirits, and write announcing his arrival to the British consul in Barcelona. He signed off: 'Trusting to see you soon.'

Alas for human perversity. Having reached Spain and freedom, with arrangements in hand for his onward passage to England via Gibraltar, Reg Miles killed himself. He was found dead in his hotel room a short distance inside the Spanish border, thus presenting historians in New Zealand and Britain with a mystery that remains unsolved to this day.

When a man of sound mind abruptly decides to kill himself, especially in such unusual circumstances, it is as mysterious as it is tragic. Despite a suicide letter and an autopsy verdict, Miles's death continues to raise questions of conspiracy and intrigue. The questions posed — 'dark actors playing dark games' — remain as puzzling as those cloaking the sudden death of Britain's chief authority on biological warfare, Dr David Kelly, in 2003.

Hero or antihero? That, I suppose, is what this story is about. Behind the conundrum lies the story of an argument, an alleged row. The row took place during a battle in the Libyan desert in North Africa at a place that is mentioned in the Bible, Belhamed. It was an argument between two men, Miles and Freyberg. Two men shouting at each other, both furious; although probably Freyberg was less furious at Miles than at the mandarins of the British Eighth Army, who had placed the New Zealand Division in an impossible situation and failed to supply it with armour. At the time, Freyberg's Division was surrounded on three sides by Rommel's tanks, with no way out except by turning tail and withdrawing from the battlefield.

As young Richard Wild, a future New Zealand chief justice but then a Divisional liaison officer, would write in his diary:

> *I suppose the British armoured people had some reason ... The men would be all right if they had good leaders. There are too many silly soppy ninnies and brainless fools wearing British officers' uniforms and if they don't wake up they'll cost us the war.*

Wild added, 'The Englishman is the most difficult problem I've ever tried to understand.'

We shall never know what was said by Miles or Freyberg, what words were spoken, although the outcome of the row is clear enough: Miles disobeyed orders and broke ranks. This is interesting, because there is nothing I can discover in Reg's early life to suggest the future rebel and subversive.

* * *

Reginald Miles was born in Springston, Canterbury, of middle-class farmers — uncomfortably middle. When he was old enough, he tells us, he was sent to a small state school, where he had his mouth washed out with soap and was bullied 'vilely' by the other boys who were the roughest of the rough. He was five or six. Possibly he was sickly, a bit of a weed, but it seems more likely that he was set upon for his manners and his accent, which he came by honestly. Reg's father, William, born in England at Gravesend, was a gentleman farmer who inherited a sizeable estate with horses and stabling, and then fell on hard times, and ended up working for the SPCA. Reg's mother, Mary, had to take in boarders. She scrimped and saved to put Reg through school.

Reg was the youngest of six children, and the only one who progressed beyond Standard Six. Until he won a scholarship to high school he paid his way, boarding with a farmer, harvesting, milking cows, cleaning boots, mucking out with horses and riding his bicycle seven miles to school and back, all for 'six bob a day'.

The bullying, he says, left him with a deep inferiority complex which would last a lifetime. So? So Reg was insecure and different from other boys. History is full of insecure men who became natural leaders. Think of

Napoléon. It's not difficult to see where his dreams and aspirations might lead him.

The farmer whom Reg boarded with as a schoolboy owned a Purdey shotgun and taught Reg to shoot; at Rangiora High School, he was a drill instructor and subaltern in the senior cadets; he may have been a crack shot — he doesn't say — but he certainly liked ceremony. For someone who was fond of reading and was a bit of a loner, progression to a place like Duntroon — where ceremonial matters and duty to the flag were sanctified as almost Kantian imperatives — was logical. Duntroon and the army would wrap the young Reg and his complexes around in a feather blanket. He loved the army. Regimental life, the discipline and the whole living organism, would prove all he could have wished for. The quirks would appear later: unpredictability, and a tendency to kick the rule book if things went wrong; that's to say, if they didn't go as he thought they should, forgetting he had written most of the rules himself.

'To be, or not to be?' (Shakespeare) — 'To obey, or not to obey?' (Nelson) — 'England expects' (Lord Nelson again, and also, by way of anecdote, Miles's headmaster). The headmaster at Rangiora High School recognised a lad of modest aspirations who would probably have come to nothing, he said, except for one thing. Reg had 'an immodest sense of duty'.

* * *

This goes some way to explain the paradox of what happened at the battle of Belhamed, which took place in November 1941 shortly after the argument with Freyberg. What did Miles do? He forgot everything he'd learned at Duntroon and jumped ship; he broke ranks and joined in the fighting alongside his men. It's a lovable trait really, except that on this occasion he was careless enough to get captured by the enemy. Naturally, Freyberg, when he heard, was furious all over again. He'd lost his best man, the heir-apparent. There you have it.

The battle of Belhamed was a turning point. It was the final battle in an epic campaign which the British had all but squandered, and the Axis general Rommel would have won if Miles hadn't been so contrary. The Cheyenne and Crow Indians have a name for people like that: they call them 'the contraries', crazy dogs wishing to die. I'm painting with a broad brush, you understand; I'm exaggerating a bit — Miles wasn't alone in stopping Rommel. Someone said he was armed only with a swagger stick of polished blackthorn. That's another exaggeration. He was carrying a Lee-Enfield rifle.

Enough of preambles. We'll never know what he said in the row with Freyberg, any more than we shall know what was in his mind when he courted death and gave himself up to the enemy. It's a fair guess, however (shame and humiliation being what they are to an officer who surrenders) that the incident preyed on his mind. Who knows? There is no way of knowing the effect that trouble may have on a man.

* * *

Miles was a gunner. According to his fellow gunner Spud Murphy — the historian W.E. Murphy — Miles became a gunner by accident. When Reg entered Duntroon, it seems he had little idea where he was going or what he wanted to do, except that the idea of rapid promotion must have appealed. Promotion meant good pay, which seemed a just reward for all the learning that was being pumped into him. (Doctrina vim promovet — Learning Promotes Strength — was the college motto.) Probably the cavalry appealed to him, but this demanded a minimum income far above his means.

He entered Duntroon in the Australian Capital Territory in 1911, within months of its being founded, writing home to his mother that the place was closer in looks to a prison camp than a college. After being sworn in, he was told by the Commandant that he was being trained for 'bloody wars and promotion', and that he would be brought back by the police if he attempted to run away.

'I rather liked that,' Miles would later confide to his wife.

Duntroon was modelled on two famous institutions, Sandhurst and West Point, and was the creation of Lord Kitchener of Khartoum, one of Reg's heroes. Kitchener had visited New Zealand in a blaze of publicity when Reg was still at school. What impressionable schoolboy could have resisted a call to Empire from that hypnotic stare, set in a face weathered by years of soldiering, the personification of British masculinity and military glory? Reg's other hero was Scott of the Antarctic. The latter appealed for a quite different reason.

'I do feel I share many of his [Scott's] weaknesses — irascibility, lack of self-confidence, moodiness etc,' he wrote. That was written from a prison camp when Reg was fifty, shortly before he died.

Kitchener and Scott. Two legendary and ill-fated men, yet opposites: the ramrod and the willow, the tough and the tender-hearted. Together, they seem to epitomise the ambivalence in Miles that is at the heart of his character. Twin poles warring inside him. It's a nice conundrum, like Duntroon itself, which taught its officer-class cadets the value of distance and restraint. In other words, 'composure' in battle. Evidently Reg was a model pupil. He learned the lesson — soon to be tested at Gallipoli — of understanding the need to get things right, while knowing that inevitably they would go wrong.

At Duntroon he passed all of his exams and went off to enlist in the infantry. This at least was the plan, but in May 1914 an epidemic of some kind swept the college. It was probably meningitis, or encephalitis. At the time of the epidemic, Miles, quarantined for a week, developed what he later called 'brain fever'. His hair began to fall out. At this stage, two-thirds of the way through his four-year course, he wrote that he might be posted anywhere — Ordnance? Signals? Engineers? He had a hidden longing to be a gunner it seems, but this didn't descend on him until later. 'Hanged if I know what to think,' he wrote to his mother.

Then came the declaration of war. In the general excitement, his course was shortened. Duntroon's entire first intake was graduated in advance and rushed overseas.

Miles graduated — a wish realised — as a regular force officer in the artillery, but then, arriving back in New Zealand, he fell ill and the artillery sailed without him. Determined to get away, he got an infantry berth in the Canterbury Battalion. At the last minute the government expanded the expeditionary force by raising a new howitzer battery, and he joined it. He got into the artillery after all.

'A great stroke of luck [for us],' Spud Murphy writes. Miles landed at Gallipoli with two 4.5 howitzers, a cannon highly prized (the name derives from 'catapult') for its ability to fire shells straight up over the steep razor-backed hills that confronted the Anzacs in the Dardanelles. It also fired high explosive besides shrapnel, whereas the 18-pounders fired primarily shrapnel.

A raw but excited Lieutenant Miles and his No. 1 troop landed at night under the command of a major in charge of a battery of four guns which were to be in action the following day. At midnight, following the infantry, the first gunners were ordered ashore. It was raining and pitch dark. Miles's two guns were taken out of the hold and lowered into the pontoons, limbered up on the beach, then dragged by hand up the hill and into the scrub and ravine. The beach already a mélée of torn and running men, an avalanche of mortar shells and small-arms fire; Reg in his tin helmet sending out runners to find gunpits and dugouts. Suddenly the ground shook; the night erupted in a sea of stabbing flames. The first howitzer had opened up. It was beyond Reg's station to give the order, but it seems he couldn't wait.

Reg's troop was in the first wave to land at Anzac Cove in April 1915, and his (legend has it) was the first salvo fired on that beach, ahead of the Australians. 'I just wanted to let our chaps know we were here,' he said.

He described the landing in a letter home to his parents. He wrote:

> *The infantry rushed the trenches 40 yards away, got too far ahead and had to retreat. Capt. Hill, in charge of my old platoon, was shot through the mouth, Barclay killed ... In the brigade were four Duntroon men, Smith, Paterson, Brooke and Selby — the first 3 were killed the first day, and Selby has since lost his right arm.*

Gallipoli. Anzac Cove. Two names lodged in the consciousness of a small nation finding its feet — and losing a great many of its sons — in pursuit of an adventure about to turn into an agonising failure. But to a gunnery officer of twenty-two, writing home from a hospital bed some months later, those early days were almost indecently satisfying. Occasionally, we read, he would order a few rounds to be fired at an invisible enemy — a Turkish gun that was getting 'obnoxious'.

Much of the time he was snug in an OP (observation post), listening for gun flashes and marking fields of fire, when not reading his mail 'while bullets rattled into the parapet'. His post was a dugout roofed with the lids of ammunition boxes, covered with waterproof sheets and lined inside with sacking — smelly, but 'luxurious'. Whenever Johnny Turk took a break, Reg went bathing off a pier by the beach early in the morning ('it is quiet and beautiful when there is no shelling'). That was about as obnoxious as it got. From the day he ordered his first salvo fired in April 1915, until the guns fell silent and the peninsula was evacuated in December, 'they were never moved and they were never hit'.

In July, he was made a captain. Three days later, on a Sunday morning, he was hanging out his blankets when he was shot by a Turkish sniper. 'Nothing serious,' he reported to his parents. 'Two slight wounds, but one in the jaw very uncomfortable.'

He had been putting out his blankets to air in the same place every morning for nearly two months. But this proved 'once too often'. The sniper's bullet fired from about 600 yards went through the jaw just under the stooping Miles's mouth, 'through my right breast making a flesh wound, missing a big vein and missing my arm altogether. I got a terrible fright.'

He spent two days almost choking, unable to speak, and was evacuated to Lesvos, then to hospital in Malta, then England. However, he was back again, reporting for duty with his captain's pips up, in time to learn that in his absence his dugout had been honoured with a visit by Lord Kitchener. Miles's post on Walker's Ridge was the only one Kitchener inspected. The great man landed at Gallipoli in November, and left recommending what seemed to be about to happen: a complete evacuation of the peninsula. Miles was disappointed. He had grown attached to his cannon and, like another young casualty called Freyberg, had returned from hospital raring to go.

Bernard Freyberg was also serving near Gallipoli, but with the English. Shot in the stomach and evacuated to Egypt in June, Freyberg was back at Helles with his battalion by 19 August, prompting a remark by an Australian nursing sister: 'I guess he's made of India rubber.' Freyberg was already famous for his night swim at Bulair; he would go on to win the Victoria Cross in 1916, and by the end of the war acquire another half-dozen wounds — nine in all —

earning him the sobriquet of 'a human colander'. Miles, of course, wounded only four times, can't compete, but, in terms of braving danger when hot lead is looking for you in battle, he and 'Tiny' Freyberg are remarkably similar.

Winston Churchill's famous phrase likening Freyberg to a salamander — 'the Salamander of the British Empire' — recalled the fire in the man, although at the time Freyberg had to inquire what a salamander was. Only later when he consulted a fortune-teller did he fully understand what Churchill meant: fire was his element. Miles, a Sagittarius born on 10 December, came by it naturally. His horoscope reads: *Fire is your element. Yours is the only zodiac sign connected with fire which like an unchecked flame burns within you.*

Freyberg's attitude to danger is well known. He scorned it, giving briefings in the field in view of the enemy while being shot at, as he would at Belhamed under fire from Rommel's tanks. Miles likewise scorned heroics. In Flanders he would be recommended for the Victoria Cross, having already won the Military Cross on the Somme, and at the end of the war in 1918 be singled out for special mention by the British Commander-in-Chief, Haig.

Twenty years on, in 1938, his daughters, growing up in New Zealand, will beg him to write something for them about his life. He will put together a 3000-word memoir, *Reginald Miles — His Story*. 'Really not worth the telling,' he says. The war is barely mentioned. He writes about money worries and about poverty, he writes about bringing up four strong-willed girls as a solo father between the wars, he writes about his father being swindled by loan sharks in Canterbury, and he mentions the First World War once. He admits to being wounded at Gallipoli and Ypres ('but not badly. Damned frightened nearly all the time!') And that's it. That's all he says. It wasn't 'a particularly bad time'. He makes the war to end wars sound almost pleasant.

Life loses its flavour, Freud said, when the highest stakes in the game of living, life itself, may not be risked. In Miles's dismissal of what it was like to be under fire — of seeing his men deafened and blinded in the trenches and vomiting from fear and revulsion at the sight of their mates disintegrating in front of their eyes, spewing their bodily parts over their lower legs and feet sunk up to the ankles in mud — we begin to see how military academies like Duntroon work, reducing slaughter and the conduct of war to a set of rules and procedures, and implanting an officer-class irony to drain the subject-matter of emotion and keep it at a distance. Which may suggest that, when we look at a photograph of the uniformed Reginald Miles, with the imperturbable toothbrush smile of the Chocolate Soldier, what we are seeing is a mask. Behind this mask — it's a question as much as a statement — is perhaps the face of 'a happy warrior'.

Two examples. Consider Bernard Freyberg, going into battle in France for the first time. Looking around, noting the situation, and reportedly saying to his regimental sergeant-major: 'Well, I think today we'll need to get ourselves a VC.' And proceeding to do just that.

Consider Reginald Judson, an infantryman from the north of Auckland who on enlisting gave his occupation as a bootmaker. In 1918, Sergeant Judson was in action in France on the Somme. At Hébuterne, at Bucquoy and at the second battle of Bapaume, Judson led attacks on enemy positions under withering fire, any one of which ought to have ended his life. He actively sought death, but won three medals instead — the Victoria Cross (VC), the Distinguished Service Medal (DSM) and the Military Medal (MM) — and lived to tell the tale.

Miles's performance in the Ypres Salient will be less spectacular, but his tempting of fate and casual courting of death, the hallmarks of a happy warrior, are of a similar order. Having said that, I am a little suspicious of myself calling him 'happy'. The picture he draws for his daughters of his own family — of a father going from job to job and ending up a dog inspector, two brothers and three sisters nearly ruined by war, the flu pandemic and the Depression — is not cheering. His eldest sister, he adds, drowned herself. 'A jaundiced and sometimes miserable man' is a snap view of Miles by the historian Christopher Pugsley. Myself, I'd say he had a gay spirit and a desolate nature (an association more common than you might think).

* * *

In 1917, at the age of twenty-four, Miles was promoted major and given charge of a howitzer battery, and posted to the low-lying, glutinous soil of Ypres. We are told that the morale of his men suffered, according to his moods. Still, it was a long war.

The Ypres Salient is in Belgium. It is a tiny battlefield in Flanders, just north of, and in a continuous line with, the long, meandering front of the Somme battlefields in France. This part of Belgium, with its rolling flatlands of hops and its spinneys of larch, already the scene of ferocious fighting in three earlier battles, had been reduced to shattered farms and ruins by the time Miles and his battery arrived under British command at the end of 1917. There would be no victories for the British at Ypres, though. It was a place of memories: first, of a legendary Christmas truce in 1914 when the two sides, German and British, stopped fighting for twenty-four hours and marked the occasion by singing carols together and playing football in a village called Ploegsteert. Ploegsteert — 'Plugstreet' to the British tommy — is the place where the phenomenon of 'trench warfare' began and where poison gas was first used. It is there that a young Winston Churchill in 1915 saw action on the edge of a mutilated wood — Churchill went out into no-man's-land thirty-six times. It is also the place where John McCrae, a Canadian doctor and artillery officer, in action during the second battle of Ypres wrote:

In Flanders fields the poppies blow
Between the crosses, row on row,
That mark our place; and in the sky
The larks still bravely singing, fly
Scarce heard amid the guns below …

Altogether there would be five battles of Ypres.

Miles was still at Duntroon at the time of the first battle in 1914. He was on the Gallipoli peninsula at the time of the second. I forget where he was at the time of the third,

Passchendaele in 1917, but he would be there in time for the fourth, the battle of the Lys. There, the German spring offensive almost succeeded in capturing Ypres and pushing the British Expeditionary Force back to the channel ports and out of the war.

Since Passchendaele, the Salient had been relatively peaceful. It was now silent. You could hear the sounds of the cuckoo and the nightingale in Ploegsteert Wood, just south of Ypres, which was still occupied by troops of the British First Army, of which Miles and his battery of five howitzers and 120 men were a part.

The First Army was a relatively weak force; its worn-out formations had been sent to a supposedly 'quiet sector'. They included, besides British, New Zealand, Australian and Belgian troops, two Portuguese divisions which were undermanned, short of officers, deficient in morale, and were about to be replaced on the same day that Ludendorff, the German commander, launched his attack with eight German divisions.

The attack began with a bombardment on the line between Armentières and Festubert, as Miles was tidying up his dugout two or three kilometres further north by Nightingale Hill, or Hill 63 as it was known, and getting ready for bed.

The Salient was the most British sector of the entire Western Front, with beer in the 'rest' villages, football in the open fields, and an English school for the children of the war graves gardeners. As well as being the most tommified sector — Plugstreet for Ploegsteert, Wipers (Ypres), Ham and Tears (Armentières), 'Hyde Park Corner' — it was also the wettest part of the line, where some men, sucked into the mud, drowned before they could be pulled out.

Between Ypres and Armentières, water is found everywhere close to the surface; in places the trenches became miniature canals and had to be constructed of sandbag barricades instead. There were few heights, and those there were were in German hands. Rising over Ploegsteert village and Hyde Park Corner was Hill 63, tree-clad, beautiful, 63 metres high, against one shoulder of which was the enemy, while occupying a scratch position behind a ridge, up against the south-eastern corner, was Miles's 6th Battery. The two sides were almost within conversational distance.

As the 1917–18 winter turned to spring, Miles was beginning to feel eerily exposed. The entire Salient was exposed, fenced off as it was on three sides by concrete pillboxes belonging to the enemy. This is why a frustrated Ludendorff, having failed in his offensive further south on the Somme, should now divert his attentions to the north against a denuded Flanders. It was the weakest part of the line.

I have never been in a battle; I have never fired a shot in anger. But I know from my reading and talking to ex-infantrymen that to be slap in the middle of events is no guarantee that you understand them; you are stuck in a shrieking, gas-blinding, chaotic situation with little knowledge and no perspective of what is going on around you.

It is said that while twenty days are enough to train an infantry man, it takes a year to make a gunner. A gunner is able to take on almost any role in the regiment. He gets an overview. The role of a gunner officer is usually to support another combat arm. He is always working one level up — a lieutenant with a captain, a captain with a major. By this stage Miles, a major, is already at brigade level with the colonel. He knows where the enemy snipers are posted and which formations — like the New Zealand rifle and machine-gun battalions strung over the flat ground west of Ypres, alongside the Portuguese — are most vulnerable. He can see the bigger picture. So when his battery is caught in the whirlwind and is overrun by the German Fourth Army, and all around is chaos with soldiers in retreat and gas raining down, he knows, insect though he is in the scheme of things, how important it is to hold his corner and to keep his head when all about him are losing theirs. At least that's what his commendation for the Distinguished Service Order tells us.

Up until March, the winter boredom has been relieved only by an attack of venereal disease (among Kiwis the infection is said to be 'greater than in any other overseas force'). With the coming of spring and the ecstasy of the first gleam of sunshine, Miles is longing for 'a little extra risk'. His wishes will soon be met. In the first thirty-five minutes of the coming bombardment, more shells will be fired, it has been calculated, than in the whole Boer War.

His guns, he says, 'are not nearly far enough forward'.

All winter he had been struggling to keep up morale. In the dugouts, hot tea froze in minutes, bully-beef became chunks of red ice. Again and again we wonder at the resilience of the men around him, enveloped by cold and mud and living in wet clothes next to bare earth, where vermin — beetles, ants, caterpillars, greenfly, lice and mosquitoes whose bites could blow up a man's face to the size of a football — were inescapable. Small wonder that when he is back in New Zealand being assessed for potential active service again, we read how his mood swings in the Salient were reflected in the morale of his battery, which was up and down, seeming to indicate he already had black depressions by then.

On 20 March, he survives an attack by mustard gas shells lobbed into his dugout. Two of his fellow officers are taken out, badly gassed. He moves to a new bivvy, his telephone lines and forward observation posts within hail of enemy pillboxes — 'Huns on our immediate right.'

On 31 March, it is 'raining steadily,'

Gas shells all morning. None of our bivvies gas-proof or even decently splinter-proof, so we didn't enjoy it much.

1 April
Bad tummy all night. Must have got a mouthful of gas. Gunners affected — can't even pick up their aiming points. Carrying out harassing fire nightly.

4 April
[Colonel] advocates putting the guns right alongside the pillboxes. If the guns get strafed, we all get it. Can't say I like the spot greatly.

6 April
Toothache. Rode to Bailleul looking for a dentist, found it a city of the dead. Absolutely forsaken. Orders received 6 p.m. to pull out of action. Everybody pleased at the prospect of going down south.

The next day the orders are countermanded, and he is told to relieve an Australian brigade.

7 April
Took over Australian guns in my old position [in Ploegsteert Wood]. Two guns in the hedge and 3 others in deep dugouts nearby. Accommodation the filthiest I have ever seen. However they make good funk holes.

8 April
Rain and mush
Shooting at trench mortars … but 100 yards short.

9 April
Big noise on our right from 4 a.m. onwards. Managed to register in 3, 4 & 5 guns, but light

poor. When I got back heard Huns had broken through and taken Bac-St-Maur ...

It is the start of a series of breakthroughs which will take the Germans almost to within sight of the channel ports. The other British guns are withdrawing. Miles has already retreated from the Messines sector in the north to the Ploegsteert area, and is told to expect orders to pull back further the next day. But the teams coming for his howitzers miss their guide and he is left, isolated.

10 April
Wakened at 3.15 a.m. by fairly heavy bombardment. Went up & found shells and gas coming over. Started firing at 1 round a minute with gas masks on. Shortly after daylight carried on at 2 rounds a minute. Wires cut, Sgt Wilson wounded — soon after 6 a.m. reports of infantry running back down the road ...

In fact they are fleeing past his guns in thick fog, with high explosive and gas raining down. Miles, armed with a swagger stick, rounds up the stragglers, mans a fire trench and halts the enemy. He returns to his guns, only one of which is still firing — ‘No 5 got a direct hit, Sgt Hendle,

Murphy and Williams killed, Smith wounded' — sends off the wounded and begins to read a series of reports which tell him the Germans are in the Catacombs (deep shelters) and also the wood.

'Didn't realise Huns so near,' he says.

His ammunition is now exhausted. He receives orders to get the guns out immediately. However, finding an Australian sergeant wandering about with a herd of dazed tommies, he orders them to follow him and plunges into the wood stiff with Germans. He returns from this reconnaissance jaunt with some valuable information, then remembers, as if by afterthought, that he is supposed to have withdrawn. But his guns, which he refuses to leave to the enemy, are sunk in mud.

About 9am, having managed by a supreme effort to get one gun halfway up to a railway siding, he goes back to extricate another, stands up to give an order and, predictably — well, it was bound to happen — is shot at close range by a sniper. He is put on a hospital ship, and two days later, on 12 April 1918, 'on a beautiful starry morning', reaches Dover.

A week later he learns of the British retreat from Passchendaele. By the end of the month, with the British Expeditionary Force all but broken, the Germans have withdrawn from the field. Their spring offensive has collapsed, at a cost of 200,000 losses.

Miles's action in the Salient is a tiny affair. On the overall face of battle, it's a pimple. He will be decorated nonetheless. 'For conspicuous gallantry', the citation reads:

> *New Zealand Force*
> MAJ. REGINALD MILES, M.C., NZ Fd. Artillery
> *For conspicuous gallantry and devotion to duty. He fought his battery until the enemy were within 500 yards and his ammunition exhausted, at the same time rallying infantry stragglers and manning a fire trench. Then made a reconnaissance into a wood sending back valuable information. He was finally wounded by rifle fire at close range.*
> (*London Gazette*, 23 July 1918)

Recommended for a VC, he is awarded the Distinguished Service Order (DSO) instead. That's less important. We remember Miles's conduct for another reason. He disobeys orders. He does what no officer in command should ever do: he abandons his post and joins in the fighting. In the words of Spud Murphy, he performs an action that is 'both brilliant and prophetic'.

Ypres, in other words, is a portent. It bears an uncanny resemblance to what will happen in Miles's final appearance twenty-three years later at Belhamed.

* * *

In England that summer, Miles met the King. He was reunited with his wife, and was back in the line in France in time for the Armistice.

He was put in plaster at Brockenhurst, the New Zealand military hospital in Hampshire. His wife, Zita, came to see him nearly every day, and taught him to knit. He had met Aimée Zita Donnelly, a demure eighteen-year-old with a peach-blossom complexion, in Australia when he was at Duntroon. She had followed him overseas. They were married in Egypt. She would bear him a son and four daughters.

He walked in the woods behind the hospital with Zita, and taught his small son, Reginald, nicknamed 'Tubby', to do jigsaw puzzles. Tubby was barely two.

Miles had been shot in the hip and arm, not badly — yet recovery was slow. There may have been some psychological damage, coupled with exhaustion, for Miles was still a bit wobbly and confused, it seems, at the time of his investiture. During the ceremony at Buckingham

Palace, the King, George V, pinned the DSO on Miles's chest, and was walking on when he stopped, arrested by something, and came back.

'Haven't we met before, major? Now when was it ...?'

'June,' blurted out Miles. (Not having, he said later, 'the faintest recollection'.)

'No, I think not. It was last January,' the King said.

The King was right. Miles had gained a Military Cross during the Battle of the Somme in December 1916; it was presented by the King in January 1917.

In the autumn of 1918, declared fit and now back at the front in France, Miles visits the graves of two Duntroon friends, Cuthbertson and Dunnett, riding out on a pony to the gunpits and dugouts of his old positions which are untouched — 'All the crosses over the graves of our men between Flers and Longueval still there, quite intact.' Altogether, a quarter of his 1911 intake at Duntroon are now no more, either killed outright or dying of wounds.

Then suddenly it is over. He is recalled to the drawing board, to plan the barrage for what will prove the last major battle of the Great War — to relieve the French town of Le Quesnoy, which is liberated from the Germans on 4 November. The mayor comes out and makes a speech. The New Zealanders who have carried the day and freed the town are decked with flowers. The French inhabitants are jubilant. A week later, on 11 November 1918, the Armistice is declared.

'Bosche gone,' Miles records in his diary, laconically.

So it is over. 'But is Germany really beaten?' he asks.

* * *

The war has given him all the experience he might have wished for. It has given him a sense of self-worth. It has not been 'a particularly bad time'. Still, it would have been nice to have won a Victoria Cross. He sounds far from jubilant, even disappointed. He looks at himself in the mirror. He is appalled by what he sees. What had remained of his hair, which he began to lose at Duntroon — remember, when he had 'brain fever'? — has fallen out. It's what arrested the King, I suppose, when he turned around at the investiture and came back. At twenty-six, Miles discovers he is quite bald.

He is seldom seen now without a hat. His dome is always covered. If he looks in the mirror, what does he see? Miles is not one to dwell on the meaning of life, although he's had plenty of time to do so. Life is full of challenges, like this business of looking in the mirror. Possibly he doesn't bother, except occasionally like a friend of mine, with a low light on in the next room: 'No hair to brush anyway, and what there is I pat into place.' Miles, I imagine, much the same. Probably he shaves by memory.

He is nonetheless beautifully shaven. The scar on his jaw where the Turkish sniper got him on Gallipoli is a tiny blemish in his otherwise regular features: oval face, toothbrush moustache, wide lips, the hint of a smile, a proud nose. He is, he seems to be telling us, looking at himself in uniform with his decorations and tabs up, remarkably handsome. He's a full colonel now. His eyes twinkle. I bet his father's didn't.

* * *

Miles's father, William, had inherited a property in Canterbury called Rainham. It had once been grand, with horses and stabling half the size of a park, where the yeoman's cavalry used to meet, but it had sunk under mismanagement and the crash of the 1880s; the inexperienced William had entrusted all of his remaining cash, which was mostly his wife's money, to an old schoolfriend, Leonard Harper. Leonard Harper was the son of Bishop Harper and a leading citizen in Christchurch;

he represented Harper & Co, the Lloyds bank of the young agricultural colony. Beware the blue blood of Canterbury! Shortly, Leonard Harper departed on a one-way trip to England, taking William's investment with him. William Miles was ruined. Reg was about eight at the time.

It was a spectacular scandal, the names of the investors who had been fleeced filling column after column in the newspaper. When the extent of the scam became known, it might have been some consolation for Reg to learn that among the unsecured investors with Harper & Co was the prime minister of England, Arthur Balfour. Balfour lost about £4000.

So amid the familiar faces of ancestors that he sees reflected in the mirror, solemn in their oval frames, there is this hidden scar recalling the naivety of his father, besides the visible one on his jaw inflicted by a Turk rifleman. Reg adored his father. He was 'a perfect English gentleman'.

Tell the truth and praise God, his father taught him. *Trust in God, not people*. Reg took the lesson to heart. He was a faithful churchgoer and communicant, and he put his trust in the army. So far it hadn't let him down.

His daughters said that he was a stern disciplinarian. I expect if he took them on holiday camping, he wouldn't let them brush their teeth or go swimming until they'd first got the tent squared, absolutely, the corners and guy-ropes and pegs tightened to the last millimetre. He must have loved them quite a lot, though, because after his wife died he took all four daughters with him to London when he was seconded to the War Office and selected for the Imperial Defence College. His wife, the lovely Zita, was hit by the 1918 flu pandemic and later had a breakdown. She never properly recovered, and died in 1936 of septicaemia.

Between the wars he kept up with developments. In 1923, he attended the staff college in Camberley, a plum assignment. He keeps getting selected for courses: a rising star in a peacetime officer's cap. Always wearing a cap.

That's probably enough about between-the-wars. He must have been quite special to get picked for Camberley. On the other hand there weren't that many regulars to choose from, not thinking ones. Compulsory training had been abolished in 1930 in New Zealand, and the army, apart from a few regular officers and a scratch force of 500, had all but gone out of existence.

In England he sounds a bit wild. 'What is to be done with Miles?' reads one report. 'Is he to be sent back to his own country?' The answer is a resounding 'yes'. He seems to have shone in everything but 'tact'. Sensitive to slights, he doesn't take kindly to being put upon. In other ways, like logistics, he is obviously something of a wizard, and back in New Zealand on the eve of the Second World War, he is far and away the best artillery man for the top job.

So much for preliminaries. Fast-forward to Greece.

* * *

When he leaves for the Second World War, in 1940, however, it is not his officer's cap he is wearing, but a trilby hat. Seen off at the quay by his daughters, two on each arm, he is in civilian dress — tie, white shirt, pressed suit, and wide-brimmed trilby. He is wearing a shiny raincoat and looking aggressively cheerful, with the hat pulled down hard like one of those hard-boiled detective types created by Dashiell Hammett. He has reason to be cheerful, for he's now a brigadier. Brigadier Reginald Miles, DSO, MC and Bar. He has risen to high command, almost on a par with Freyberg, although why he should be in disguise (he sailed under the assumed name of 'Mr Mills') is anyone's guess. Maybe it's a throwback to those feats of derring-do captured in the sticky coloured plates of the *Boy's Own* magazines he read as a schoolboy? Anyway he's a good stand-in for Hammett's Sam Spade in *The Maltese Falcon*. It's the trilby that does it.

The only photograph I have seen of him without a hat was taken by the Spanish police. It is fastened to his death certificate by a rusted paper clip. There are a few wisps of hair visible about the bare dome and temples. The eyes are strange. They are strange in the way of men whose invulnerability to fear under shelling has been haemorrhaging and has finally departed, leaving only a peculiar blankness under the lids. It's quite scary, because, like the emperor in his new clothes, we don't recognise the man inside the face at all. The photograph must have been taken on the day he died, or the day before he died.

The image of him I like most was taken two years earlier in the desert. It shows a burly, muscular figure with his sleeves rolled up and a thrust in the shoulders. In the background, men in shorts are preparing one of their ritual brew-ups of tea, bivouacking. Miles wears a crumpled armband and cap. The armband says 'CRA' (Commander Royal Artillery). He is relaxed and smiling. The picture radiates great warmth and helps to explain how 'with his great physical strength' he inspired his men in Flanders to superhuman efforts to free their guns stuck in mud.

* * *

He reaches England in 1940. He is still building up the artillery; it will take him two years. When war breaks out in 1939, New Zealand doesn't possess a single anti-tank weapon. Guns are no longer horse-drawn, new equipment is scarce, motor transport limited, the available ordnance is obsolete and, with the shift in emphasis from static trench warfare to mobility, the whole gunnery game has changed. It is only when he gets to England — he's been put in charge of the Kiwi infantry brigade diverted from the Middle East to help safeguard the British coastline, which is under threat of invasion — that he begins to fill some of the gaps.

'What a shower,' he comments. He is not talking about the weather but of those enlisting in Britain to join 34 (NZ) Battery of 7 Anti-Tank Regiment, when the scare of invasion has passed and the brigade is about to sail and rejoin the Division in Egypt. They include architects, musicians, gardening students 'and odd specialists such as a floor manager from a Lyons Corner House, a colonial servant from North Borneo, idealists from the Spanish War and a cook from the Savoy Hotel'.

Altogether he will create a divisional artillery half the size of a small army, with seventy-two field guns (25-pounders) and assorted anti-tank and light anti-aircraft weapons, totalling over 4000 men conveyed in some 600 vehicles, and a headquarters numbering fifty-four all ranks. He is still training it when the New Zealanders are diverted again, this time to Greece.

The disaster on the Greek mainland and subsequent loss of the island of Crete in 1941, two military defeats in a row, are well documented, although not always the role of the artillery. Miles will miss the battle for Crete altogether.

He lands on the Greek mainland with only medium guns, 18-pounders, no match for German armour pouring down from the north. Yet his gunners save the day at the Piniós gorge in the retreat from Olympus, and hold the pass at Thermopylae where Freyberg is fighting a rearguard action under constant air attack.

'Fire until you drop,' Miles orders at the Thermopylae crossroads, the last pass before Athens. He must have been pleased with his men. A report from the German side, which has overwhelming superiority on the ground and in the air, reads: 'Unexpected and extremely heavy opposition. Enemy artillery firing like mad.'

But Miles is worn-out, on the point of collapse. He has been without sleep for a period of four days and four nights. He is evacuated to Crete on 25 April 1941, takes temporary command of the New Zealand troops already on the island, then hands over to Freyberg three days later. Freyberg lands on 28 April and immediately sends Miles to hospital in Egypt to convalesce. We don't hear from him again until Libya.

* * *

The desert war in Libya, fought by the Allies against first the Italians and then, with the arrival in North Africa of Rommel's panzers, against the German armoured divisions plus the Italians, would last three years. It might have been over in a few months if a man called O'Connor, another unlucky warrior, had had his way. Dick O'Connor would be one of the last to see Miles alive.

Sir Richard Nugent O'Connor was an audacious British general who in 1940, when the war was young, was in command of an absurdly small British force which almost completely destroyed a much larger Italian army in the Western Desert. All might have been well if Winston Churchill had not, as one of his biographers remarked, 'stuck his nose in'. O'Connor had a series of victories over the Italians. He chased them as far as Benghazi, and wanted to press on. He would have driven the enemy out of Africa altogether, but Churchill minuted from London, '*Hold*

Benghazi. Stay put.' And O'Connor, silly man — he never forgave himself afterwards — obeyed.

I am paraphrasing the British prime minister, but that in essence is what Churchill minuted to his high command in Cairo on 12 February 1941, on the very day that Rommel and his Afrika Korps, sent to rescue the Italians by a panicky Hitler, landed in Tunisia. The rest, as they say, is history. Forgive the diversion. We shall meet O'Connor again.

The other man who will have a bearing on Miles's fate, another general, is Godwin-Austen. Lieutenant-General Godwin-Austen is the Commander of 13 Corps, Eighth Army, of which the New Zealand Division in the campaign that is about to begin is a part. The campaign, called 'Crusader', will last seventeen days: a series of battles beginning on 15 November 1941 and ending on 1 December, the day Miles is captured. More than 1000 tanks and a cast of 250,000 will be involved, in a setting the size of Italy. In my atlas, the campaign map covers half the top of Africa. There were no front lines.

Crusader has been described as the strangest encounter of the entire desert war: a campaign of attrition without parallel. It would end in a genuine victory for the British, a harbinger of Allied triumphs to come. That is the good part. The rest is open to question.

Godwin-Austen sums it up: 'The story of this campaign is simple. Freyberg and the New Zealanders broke the Afrika Korps but in doing so destroyed themselves.'

It began well enough. Freyberg, having rebuilt his division after the Greek calamity, has transformed it from an embryo citizens' army to a professional fighting unit. The Division travels by night in a vast column stretching for 25 miles. It crosses the wire from Egypt into Libya and takes the enemy by surprise. It captures a major Italian fort and other strongpoints and consolidates the gains, before moving on across the uncharted desert heading for Tobruk on the north coast. It is following in the wake of the British Eighth Army. Auchinleck, the commander-in-chief, has two aims: to relieve the beleaguered Allied garrison at Tobruk, under siege for months, and to drive the Germans out of Africa. Already reports are coming back of British successes ahead and to the north.

Miles's field regiments — they are equipped now with 25-pounders, effective against both tanks and longer-range targets — are performing well, although for the first sixteen days Miles is silent. He has left us nothing in writing. But come with me to meet Steve Weir of the 6th Field Regiment. He writes: 'We were treated to the most wonderful action, and from time to time were presented with targets I never even dreamed about.' Colonel Weir is Miles's lieutenant, a master gunner in the making. He has been with Miles in Greece, and has managed to ship his guns back to Egypt more or less intact. Crusader will be the making of him; he will be there at the finish and escape capture himself by a whisker.

'You have no idea,' Weir goes on, describing to his brother in New Zealand an attack by five German panzers, 'how effective the 25-pounder is against tanks. But my guns put an armour-piercing shell through the leader, leaving it a blazing mass, to incinerate the crew. The remainder made off.'

It is four days later. Already the picture has changed. Excitement in the Division has turned to dismay on learning that reports of British successes further ahead are false. In three days of fighting, the Eighth Army has lost 530 tanks to the enemy's 100. Rommel, with a force of eight divisions, three of which surround the besieged city of Tobruk, has seized the initiative. This he will maintain for five days, until 28 November.

Most of the British losses occur in and around two ridges, the escarpments of Sidi Rezegh and Belhamed. Together they control the corridor which leads to the pocket around Tobruk. It is here one Sunday morning that Miles and Weir look down from the higher of the two ridges, Sidi Rezegh, onto the outer defences of Tobruk in the distance. Weir wonders aloud 'if we would join hands'.

In fact they will. They do. After a week's nonstop fighting, with the command structure of Eighth Army in virtual collapse, Freyberg, with two brigades supported by a battalion of tanks, sets out to achieve what five English and South African brigades have failed to accomplish; and eventually, after a series of night attacks, he succeeds in punching a hole in the defences and linking up with Tobruk. He is able to do this because Rommel has lost his head. In an insane move, intended to deliver an all-out blow to the Eighth Army and replenish his supplies and ammunition, Rommel has departed the scene in an inexplicable dash to the frontier wire. It is this mistake that allows Freyberg to open the corridor to Tobruk — but there is a price. As Chris Pugsley says, it's a corridor 'on paper only'. Realising his mistake, Rommel comes charging back, intent on annihilating the New Zealand Division.

We now come to a peculiar mindset. It's a British mindset. It is called the 'cowpat theory'. I should have mentioned it before, but there is a lot to take in. Freyberg has three brigades. He needs all three to hold the corridor, but has only two brigades with which to do it. The third has been amputated and relegated to a static role some distance back, in obedience to the British doctrine of splitting rather than concentrating its forces. This is the cowpat theory of war, anathema to Freyberg and Miles, where your troop dispositions are widely spread like cowpats in a paddock, one here, one there. The result is that seven New Zealand battalions with only light armour to protect them are left isolated to face Rommel's army as it returns from the frontier.

By now, Godwin-Austen, the Corps commander, has moved his headquarters inside Tobruk and is demanding that the corridor be kept open 'at all costs'. It's this fixation which sets the scene for the row.

The scenario is complicated. I've been trying to get my head around it. Think of a horseshoe, with the two ridges of Sidi Rezegh and Belhamed at the bottom or curved ends, and 10 or 12 kilometres away to the north Tobruk, the approaches inhabited by English, Indians, Italians, Polish, Germans, South Africans, Australians and New Zealanders, in a seesawing fog of battles. The situation is changing so rapidly that it is difficult to keep track of one's own troops, let alone the enemy's.

Sidi Rezegh has been in New Zealand hands since 26/27 November, but precariously so. Ditto Belhamed. The

20th and 21st Battalions, numbering 1300 men between them, have virtually ceased to exist, having been wiped out in the fighting. On 29 November, Rommel's tanks return from the border and begin taking up positions to the north and south of the two ridges. The Division is effectively surrounded. However, help is promised. A South African brigade, demanded by Freyberg and under his command, is reported to be on the way.

That night on Sidi Rezegh, amid the tension of waiting, Weir has gone to bed and fallen asleep, in the anticipation of 'knowing South Africa was coming up to secure our southern flank'. He wakes:

> *Roused just before midnight, to find about 500 yards away a column of vehicles, tanks, infantry in lorries, and guns, moving west going through a hole in our lines in the dark. We crept out and watched. Our guns couldn't see. As you know, we can't fire in the dark. I reported this to the Chief [Miles] who was in bed. He said, 'Let them go.' So we went back and watched this extraordinary procession fade away to the west and not a shot fired by either side.*

The promised South African brigade didn't come.

> *Sunday, 30th:*
> *A rather grim day. Fighting in the morning. Fighting in the afternoon. About 4 p.m. the Germans come out of the sun, attacking the two battalions holding Sidi Rezegh. There is a fierce battle. Then silence.*

Weir is left without infantry protection for his guns. Left defenceless, he urges Miles to have the guns withdrawn to safety inside the Tobruk perimeter. Miles agrees, realising there is no alternative. Then word comes back to Weir: 'No. We had to stay.' Miles, it seems, has been overruled. This is the setting and the presumption for the argument between Miles and Freyberg, witnessed by Spud Murphy as he was standing outside Freyberg's headquarters vehicle. He recalled 'a blazing row' between the two men.

'I heard it myself,' Murphy said. 'I don't know what it was about.' Nor do we. But we can guess.

Here are three frustrated men: Miles, Weir and Barrowclough: Barrowclough, whose brigade on Sidi Rezegh has been decimated, 'quietly angry'; Weir, 'very bitter'; Miles 'incandescent with fury' at what is to come.

All three urge Freyberg to withdraw, but in vain. That night at the last minute Freyberg sends Miles into Tobruk in an attempt to have the situation clarified.

It is night-time. Miles is lucky to survive the journey. (The British officer guiding him is killed on the way back.) Miles returns at 4.30am with a message of indecision. The British seem to believe that the New Zealanders are already 'inside the corridor'. A misunderstanding? Freyberg is ordered to hold on.

'You realise,' we can imagine Miles saying to him, 'what the consequences will be?'

'I agree,' Freyberg says in his high-pitched, squeaky voice. A bit higher and squeakier in the circumstances than usual. And that's that.

It's a tactical argument, not a personal one.

According to his critics, Freyberg on occasion can be a bit, well, slow. He even considers going into Tobruk himself. He's left it too late for that, though. Miles realises that to save the Division he will have to sacrifice his guns. Someone, I forget who, Pugsley or Murphy, claims he behaves 'as if he's got a chip on his shoulder'. Anyway, the stage is set.

* * *

There is a thick mist when Miles wakes in the morning. Correction: he is still groggy from lack of sleep, like Freyberg. Chances are he hasn't been to bed at all. He only got back from Tobruk a couple of hours ago. He can hear gunfire. Mist and fog below in the wadis. The attack has already started. He tries to reach the general by radio, but can get no sense out of Freyberg's aides. The two headquarters are half a mile from each other. They don't know what is happening either. He can't reach Weir, or Barrowclough. Then, racked with worry and ignoring the rules, unable to stand the waiting, Miles leaves his post and goes forward to be with his men.

'Goes forward' is a euphemism. He jumps in his car and crashes down the slope. The car overturns. Miles and his driver are thrown out. He arrives at Belhamed on foot, ducking the hot lead and mortar bombs showering down like rain. It is about 8.30am on Sunday, 1 December 1941. Sidi Rezegh is already lost; Belhamed is the last obstacle in Rommel's path. The opening salvo, blowing the first of Miles's 25-pounders to smithereens, had arrived with the clearing of the mist, at 7.30am precisely.

A scene of confusion. A number of men, heating primuses, are still having breakfast; others, receiving reports of tanks approaching, thinking they must be the overdue South Africans; or are limbering up, believing their guns are to be withdrawn into Tobruk. Still others, having taken up positions hastily in the dark, know so little that they have failed to lay anti-tank mines even though there are three lorry-loads at hand, and when the attack comes their guns are found to be facing the wrong way.

The opening bombardment comes in salvoes of three. Murphy describes the effect: 'compressing men in slit trenches and sucking them upwards and dropping them back' with the concussion. He describes the advance of the Afrika Korps, tanks, guns and lorried infantry neatly spaced and coordinated, the tanks using smoke grenades to blind the gun crews. The crews encumbered, their fields of fire obscured by their own vehicles charging about. In the pits, Weir's forward batteries are giving battle as fast as the shells can be rammed home, firing at gun flashes in a thickening haze too dense to penetrate. Weir is trying to direct them by radio. He sees enemy tanks with their turrets almost lifted off burst into flames and thinks, *Yes, we're getting the better of him.* He runs from battery to battery, stops during a lull, then hurries to the forward-most position. He stands stricken at the spectacle of the guns of 30th Battery, draped with bodies and caked with the flesh and blood of the men who have served them. He watches silently as the guns are put out of action, one by one.

Miles, too, is making the rounds. He is walking about, in full battledress, keeping the gunners steady. There are a number of eyewitness accounts.

'He appeared out of nowhere,' troop sergeant Wait says, 'I felt a tap on the shoulder. I looked up startled. It was the Brigadier. "*Good work, boy. Give one shell for one tank. Keep it up.*"'

He carried a light coat. He was wearing his CRA armband. He had a rifle slung over one arm, 'looking for all the world as if he was going duck shooting'.

Miles walked on, quietly encouraging his men. He paid little attention to the hail of bullets and shrapnel which filled the air, but: 'He stooped a little as the firing became more intense.'

Miles's own account, written from prison camp, describes the German infantry taking cover behind burning lorries and picking off his gunners with machine-gun and mortar fire, 'impossible to subdue'.

> *I reached the nearest gun. Then figures appeared which I saw were German infantry and I told the Lieutenant to take them on. As I spoke, No 3 gun*

> *pulled out past us and a shell struck the quad. Almost simultaneously a burst of machine-gun fire shot down Bevin [the lieutenant] and most of the crew alongside me. I was a bit dazed.*

Miles is hit. He jumps wounded into a trench and, in an uncanny replay of his action at Hyde Park Corner twenty-three years earlier, begins shooting with his rifle — 'hoping to pick off the German officer leading the infantry coming [straight at us]. Unfortunately though I waited until he got close and fired steadily I missed him! Shades of my early days as a rifle shot! The German infantry then enveloped us ...'

It was over by 2pm. Technically, Rommel had won. But it was a Pyrrhic victory: the Germans were fought to a standstill. Miles's men and 6th Brigade by their last stand had worn down the Afrika Korps to such an enfeebled degree — Rommel was down to thirty-eight tanks — that when at the eleventh hour a British tank regiment arrived in support, Rommel was obliged to accept defeat and retire west to Benghazi, deep inside Libya, leaving Tobruk at the centre of the stage still in British hands.

As one Kiwi wag put it, 'We were buggered about, and Jerry was buggered about, but we've won because we're more used to it.'

A British account paints an almost comical picture of the end.

Freyberg has been watching, encircled by tanks on three sides. He is standing near his headquarters, a solitary figure in a greatcoat looking down through a pall of smoke and machine-gun fire. He sees the tanks come right into the gun lines, slaughtering the crews and destroying the guns. He can't bear to watch, yet he can't tear himself away. He has only a skeleton headquarters left; everyone else has withdrawn inside Tobruk. His aides are starting to panic.

'Sir, if we don't go soon ...'

'Sir, I really think the moment has come ...'

It is only when he sees the gunners 150 yards away begin to put up their hands that he seems to understand the peril he is in, and agrees reluctantly to get into his vehicle. Then:

> *Twelve or fifteen soldiers got up out of the scrub and sand and clambered into and all over the staff car. There was the usual moment of doubt and then, with men festooned all over the bonnet, mudguards and boot, it wheeled about, sped past us and vanished down the Trigh Capuzzo.*
>
> (from Richard Humble, *Crusader: Eighth Army's forgotten victory*)

By nightfall, Freyberg's mauled division has extricated itself and withdrawn, and is heading back towards Egypt. Miles has been marched into captivity.

Two or three days later, a British artillery general named Latham drove across from Tobruk and inspected the battlefield, to see whether any of the guns that remained could be salvaged.

'I found poor Miles's car, on its side with his kit still in it,' he wrote.

'Practically every gun was a write-off. The dead were lying around each gun, each man nearly in his place and burned out tractors and trailers were just in rear. Here undoubtedly there had been no thought of surrender or withdrawal. The whole thing gave me the feeling of the fort in "Beau Geste" ... ' (He is recalling the epic film *Beau Geste*, in which French legionnaires were found dead at their posts, propped against the walls, after defending their fort in the Sahara against impossible odds.)

Brigadier Latham continues, 'I thought to myself: I have seen these chaps fighting for many a day now [but] something has happened here quite out of the ordinary.'

Latham was moved by what he saw. He picked up a rammer lying beside a shattered 25-pounder, and when he returned to Tobruk he had it inscribed and sent to Freyberg.

Freyberg gave it to Weir, who kept it to the end of the war to give to Miles, who of course was never able to receive it.

* * *

Bravery is a strange attribute. Winston Churchill was brave, gloriously so, but in the case of Churchill the glory and prestige that went with it were almost as important as his boisterous desire for exposing himself to danger and cheating death. 'Tiny' Freyberg was ridiculously brave, but was a man without fear, which is something else. Bernard Freyberg took courage for granted. 'I expect all my officers to be brave,' he said on one occasion, and never put a premium on the prestige he gained from his exploits. Reggie Miles was something else again. Miles was tactically brave. Buried somewhere deep within him was a desire to prove himself, and also a need to be right and be seen to be right.

Miles is more complicated than either Churchill or Freyberg, who are able to stumble and make mistakes without stopping to gnaw their innards with self-reproach. They carry on regardless. At Belhamed, Miles behaves like the First World War poet, Sassoon, at Craiglockhart. At the hospital in Craiglockhart, Siegfried Sassoon, we remember from Pat Barker's account in her *Regeneration* trilogy, is being treated by Dr Rivers for shellshock. When Sassoon insists on going back to the front, Rivers knows that it is with the intention of being killed. 'Although partly no doubt [Pat Barker writes], this was self-dramatisation: *I'll show them. They'll be sorry.*' At Belhamed, Reg Miles courts death in a similar manner. He is quivering with fury at Freyberg and the British for forcing him to sacrifice his beloved guns and gunners. Yet he has no choice. And so: *'Bugger you. I'm going to be with them at the end.'*

This, too, may be partly self-dramatisation. But underneath, as with Sassoon, Miles had, I believe, a genuine desire for death.

* * *

Miles, however, survives. He is not killed at Belhamed. All that happens is that he gets a splinter in the back from shrapnel. He is taken by the Germans and handed over to the Italians. He makes two bids to escape: the first while still in Libya being driven to board ship, when he seizes the steering wheel and attempts to overturn the car, only to collide with a lorry. The second is on the island of Crete en route to Italy. Both attempts fail. He is finally delivered in an ecstasy of frustration to a prison outside

Florence, where he arrives in late December 1941 in time for Christmas.

Miles's arrival at the fortress of Vincigliata was greeted by a select company of inmates. Vincigliata was a high-profile prison for senior officers. When Miles arrived, there were thirteen generals resident and an air marshal, two of them VCs. One of these, an engaging Nelsonian with one eye and one arm, would later be immortalised in Evelyn Waugh's trilogy, *Sword of Honour.* Another inmate, whose round face and rumpled pullover were immediately familiar, Miles recognised — '*Well, I never!*' — as belonging to an old friend and fellow South Islander, James Hargest.

Brigadier James Hargest had been in charge of Freyberg's 5 Brigade when it was overrun by Rommel at Sidi Azeiz on 27 November. He had been captured four days before Miles.

'Hello, Jimmy,' Reg said.

'Hello, Reg. Welcome to the club.' It was a joyous reunion. The two had known each other for nearly thirty years — first on the Somme in 1916, again as comrades-in-arms in the retreat from the Greek mainland defending the bottlenecks at the Olympus pass and Larissa in 1941, and finally during the Crusader campaign in the Libyan Desert just ended. Hargest was from Invercargill. He was a plain-faced jovial farmer-politician who should never, it was said, have been allowed to talk his way back into uniform when he enlisted a second time in 1939 (he had already been failed by a medical board). A squat figure whose outward appearance — he resembled a squashed dumpling — belied an individual possessed of the joys of battle. After a meteoric rise in the First World War — he was a battalion commander at twenty-seven — Hargest emerged as one of the most distinguished soldiers in the New Zealand Division. Yet twenty-two years later in the Second World War, at a critical stage in the Battle for Crete, we find a brigadier close to breakdown, plunged in apathy and indecision, and still in his pyjamas — victim of a bout of listless muddle-headedness upon which the surrender of Maleme airfield to the Germans and the subsequent loss of the entire island have been blamed. Freyberg never trusted Hargest after Maleme, which is why in the desert Hargest and his brigade found themselves in a static role behind the lines at Sidi Azeiz airfield.

Yet see how he bounces back! Come with Hargest on the road up the White Mountains. In that chaotic retreat and evacuation from Sfakia after the battle for Crete was lost, Hargest, still in the helmet issued to him at Aldershot the previous year, has regained his equilibrium and is once more the fighting commander armed with a rifle and spurring his men on.

Or see him later at the airfield in Libya with his headquarters blown to pieces by the Afrika Korps — see him, in the eyes of his biographer, Aaron Fox, 'with his rifle in the line with his troops trying to find a target to shoot at through the pall of smoke which covers the battlefield, as his soft-skinned vehicles burn out of control and the German tanks shoulder their way through the carnage'.

A more enigmatic warrior would be hard to find. James Hargest is brave and bold, testy and above self-reproach. In his immunity to criticism he is like the sundial, he recognises only the sunny hours. His self-confidence is irrepressible, making him of immense comfort and the ideal companion to a gentle and temperamental giant like Miles.

Hargest told Miles the castle was unheated. It was cold and damp. The regime was rigid: baths twice a week, dress for dinner. No politics or religious discussion allowed. But the company more than made up for it.

'I am ashamed of being reported wounded,' Miles wrote to his second wife, Georgie, early in 1942, when conflicting reports of his capture had begun to circulate. (Miles had appeared in technicolour on the front of an Italian magazine as a lieutenant-general with whiskers and a red-banded cap, while Hargest's capture with about 500 men had been inflated on the state wireless to a strength of 10,000.) 'They are wildly invented and not worth repeating,' he wrote to New Zealand military forces commander Lieutenant General Edward Puttick. 'Don't like the castle much, but we are fortunate and get daily walks.'

The castle walls were solid stone, the windows small, the rooms easily searched; while outside along the embrasures, under the battlements, was a perfect walk for the sentries who could look down on every square inch of ground outside the actual castle area.

Writing to his wife, Miles sounds despondent. But he has come at a time of activity, a flurry of plots being hatched in secret by an escape committee of four. Chief of the four were Adrian Carton de Wiart, the piratical gentleman already mentioned, and our old friend Major-General Sir Richard O'Connor, known as 'General Dick'. De Wiart had been knocked unconscious and captured after a plane crash near Italy. With his eye-patch and empty sleeve, the one-armed general would be a natural model for Evelyn Waugh's fire-eating fictional brigadier, Ben Ritchie-Hook. Richard O'Connor, whose brilliance put the Italians to rout in the desert, had been captured by Rommel early in the piece.

Miles, aching to return to the Division, was soon taken into O'Connor's confidence. Dick O'Connor was the quintessential escaper: he thought, dreamed, plotted and talked escape 'until his face began to show contours all over'.

O'Connor's bids for freedom had already infuriated the Italian guards. They had built 'yet another wall to confine us into a still smaller space where we can be watched more easily'.

From the outside, the castle was deceptive. It appeared enormous, with towers and ramparts, walls two-and-a-half feet thick, a moat and walled-in gardens. It was, however, a folly, and the house within, where they were confined on four floors, was quite modest. Miles and Hargest were given a room in the attic, sixty-five steps up. O'Connor explained that the castle had been rebuilt on medieval lines by an Englishman. He had restored it quite thoughtlessly, without regard to the many underground passages which he had sealed up.

'He has made things very difficult for us, Miles.'

For his fourth bid, O'Connor devised a plan involving both Miles and Hargest, besides six others to divert the attention of the sentries. Miles lifted and managed to heave the Englishman up onto the battlements and over the side.

It was night. O'Connor's belt caught in the parapet. At the last moment he was seen, and escape attempt No. 4 was foiled.

A rope was found in one of the bedrooms. The number of guards was increased, and the rooms searched twice-daily. O'Connor became depressed. Miles also. He wrote to his wife saying that food and Red Cross parcels were getting through, also books. But he didn't particularly want books. All he wanted, he said, was a Bible. But when it came, it seemed to depress him further.

'Dear Georgie,' he wrote:

> *Darlingest … I shall need your comfort and love in the days ahead when I am free. I don't know what sort of attitude I shall have to face on the part of my superiors and fellow officers …*

'Georgie' was his second wife. They were very much in love. He had married Georgette Bisset-Smith at the Scotch National Church in Westminster, London, on 31 May 1940, and bade her goodbye when he sailed for Egypt a few months later. She was much younger than him, and we assume she must have been mystified, as puzzled by what he said in his letter as we are. The letter was written in May 1942, six months after the battle for Belhamed. It was the first time he had told her about what he called his 'doubts and difficulties'. Georgie could have had no idea what he was talking about.

Miles and Hargest dug and gardened, producing peas and lettuce from the cold, damp soil. They all had hobbies to combat stagnation or depression. Hargest hunted for snails. Douglas Stirling bred rabbits, General Combe kept hens. Miles took up map-copying, then sewing. He became an expert tailor. His teacher was Lieutenant-General Sir Philip Neame, VC, a former big-game hunter whose hobby was embroidery. Neame made exquisite tapestries for chair covers. Dick O'Connor's hobby was escape-plotting, his zeal undimmed after being locked up for a month in solitary confinement. His first attempts, abetted by de Wiart, Miles and Hargest — one to cut a hole in the masonry, the other a trial tunnel abandoned when they struck solid rock — came to nothing except that a new fascist captain arrived. Security was overhauled once again, searchlights mounted by the sentry boxes, and kilometres of barbed-wire fencing were strung around the outside of the battlements. More guards arrived.

The fourteen inmates were now deploying over 200 men away from the active theatre of war.

* * *

It is said that war neurosis is a result of prolonged strain and long periods of immobility and helplessness. Any explanation, according to the writer Pat Barker, 'has to account for the fact that this apparently intensely masculine life of war and danger produced in men the same disorders that women suffered from in peace'. She writes about First World War veterans damaged by the horrors of fighting in the trenches, and what she says rings true, except that in the case of Miles we have to factor in a couple of extra things. One is his unspoken grief for the loss of his only son, 'Tubby', who had died at the age of twenty-five. He had joined the Fleet Air Arm and was killed with his squadron in 1940 when his ship, HMS *Glorious*, was attacked and sunk by German battleships off Norway. The other factor is Miles's unwillingness or inability to talk about his personal problems, despite — or because of — being surrounded by such a vintage collection of alert and perceptive minds.

'Not a solitary soul from the Middle East has written to me,' he told Georgie. 'Yet when I go over the whole affair again, as I do dozens of times every day and every night, I cannot see that I could have done anything very different from what I did.'

He seems to think he was in disgrace for his conduct at Belhamed. Nor is his friend and room-mate Jimmy Hargest able to talk Miles out of his *idée fixe* that he had done something reprehensible and would be punished for it.

Hargest was small and untidy. His shirt flaps, his bootstraps seem perennially undone. Beside him in photographs, Miles towers over him, protective, a gentle giant. They make an incongruous pair. They could not be more different. The one, slighting of himself, forever examining his motives, brave as a lion yet, according to General O'Connor, 'always producing crises'; the other, the diminutive Hargest, 'full of sound ideas' (O'Connor again), a tower of strength.

There can be no doubt of the warmth between the two companions, they are like blood brothers. Hargest, when he learns of Miles's death, will break down and cry like a baby; Miles's last letters, when he is in crisis and at his most vulnerable, express deep concern for the fate of Hargest. And yet a paradox remains. When it comes to personal problems, they seem quite unable to confide in each other.

Unexpectedly, we learn from one of Miles's letters that he has in fact plucked up courage and talked to someone. (Neame? de Wiart?) 'I have talked it over with a V.C.

general here,' he tells Georgie. 'He, at any rate, doesn't hold me blameworthy.'

Blameworthy for what? For an act of heroism? At Belhamed he had done everything he could do and he'd done it with style. Where has it got him? Is that what he's thinking? We wonder what Georgie is thinking, if she senses as we do that he may be starting to lose the thread.

But no. He's on top of things again. He has heard from Freyberg, he tells her — 'A very nice letter ... He was quite nice about it, saying "You certainly had no chance whatever."' Then, with his birthday looming: 'I shall soon be fifty. I feel fitter than I did ten years ago!'

* * *

With the arrival of spring his mood lifts again, this time for real. O'Connor and de Wiart, the two arch-plotters, have made a discovery. Having abandoned all plans of going out over the top, they have combed the interior of the castle and proposed digging a tunnel underneath the chapel, one side of which abuts on to the outside wall of the castle. The chapel is bricked-up on all sides, but de Wiart has found a way in through a disused lift well. They have dug down and begun tunnelling.

They dig for seven months. There are six of them chosen to go out: Miles and Hargest, de Wiart and O'Connor, Combe and Boyd. They dig in pairs, digging for two hours every day.

Hargest describes it in a book he will write afterwards in England: 'We had two workers and two watchers all through. When we were about six feet down the shaft, O'Connor took charge of "operations". Because of his injuries de Wiart insisted on watching both morning and afternoon during the whole period. He is one of the coolest men I have ever met, yet even his nerves were frayed by the incessant strain.'

They had a kitchen knife, a trowel and some iron bars. They moved 200 tons of rock and hid the spoil inside the chapel. They went down 10 feet, dug under the castle, the garden and the battlements, under the roadway, and came up outside in a wood. They had the services of a forger, General Gambier-Parry, a skilled artist who provided the necessary identity cards; a carpenter and joiner (Air Marshal Boyd), who kept the pit-props in the tunnel from collapsing; and a tailor (Miles), who at dead of night in his room made an illicit suit and caps and jackets from army blankets sent by the War Office, but was stumped, according to Hargest, trying to dye a pair of trousers blue.

'Reg spent nearly two months, using a mixture of walnuts, berries and Condy's crystals, without success,' Hargest related six months later to a gathering at Chatham House in London. 'Finally in desperation he made a brew of black boot polish and a bottle of ink, dropped the trousers in, and the result was marvellous.'

The six — five generals and an air marshal — crawled out of the tunnel in battle order: Combe, Miles, Boyd, Hargest, O'Connor and de Wiart. Everything went without a hitch, even to the six dummy bodies left tucked up in their beds, complete with artificial beards and hair-lines, which were not discovered by the guards until the next morning. By then Miles and Hargest were in Milan waiting for a train to Como on the Swiss border, and the other four were, it seemed, well away.

Alas for the others. Brigadier Combe was recaptured the next day in Milan, caught gazing at a railway timetable. De Wiart, disguised as an Italian peasant, opted to walk with O'Connor. Surprisingly, given their inability to speak the language and de Wiart's piratical appearance, with an eye-patch and an empty sleeve, they remained at large for seven days after walking over the Apennines. They were recaptured near Bologna.

Air Marshal Tudor Boyd, Miles's tunnelling companion,

was unlucky. He got to Milan with Miles and Hargest, lost them at the station, hid in a wagon on a train which arrived at Como by the frontier, only to be shunted tactlessly into a goods yard. Next morning, impatient for air, he climbed out and was retaken, on the edge of freedom. Only the New Zealanders were successful.

Miles and Hargest escaped on the night of 29 March 1943 dressed as workmen. They reached Como the next day. There, they walked boldly up the road to the border, to a point where they could observe the frontier fence and the mountain terrain beyond, north of Chiasso, with a view to crossing after dark. That evening they climbed into a wooded valley and clambered about, avoiding sentries. Miles knelt with a pair of wire-cutters and cut a square in the 12-foot-high security fence. As they crawled through, the fence shook and alarm bells began to jingle. They shot like rabbits into the forest beyond.

'Jim,' Miles paused for breath. He felt himself grow to three times his normal size, he recalled later. 'Jim!' he cried. 'We're in Switzerland!' Hargest, out of a lifetime of habit, looked at his watch. It was 10.30pm.

O, happy Swiss! O, happy Switzerland!

Miles loved the place, after the privations of captivity. We can imagine. The hospital air. The countryside 'almost painfully beautiful'. The rolling hills with neat, well-kept woods. Pleasant farm houses, green fields and lakes. In the distance, glorious mountains. Everything neat and scrupulously clean. And the solicitude of his hosts, Kathi and Rolf Bürgi, who took him into the quiet of their garden home at Belp, near Bern, with its elms and lawns against the white background of the Alps.

Switzerland, a bower of bourgeois bliss.

Miles had feared that they would be interned. Switzerland in 1943, though neutral, was cordoned off, surrounded by hostile Nazi and pro-Nazi regimes, and controlled by an alert Swiss police who were not always kind to the refugees who turned up on their borders. However, two middle-aged tramps purporting to be British generals were another matter. Bully for them! They were given coffee, locked in a cell with straw pillows and mattresses, next morning more coffee, then, having promised not to speak to anyone, were taken by their plainclothes police escort to visit a couple of historic castles. The Swiss police were charming. They passed them on to the British legation in Bern, where the military attaché, Henry Cartwright, received them gladly. Cartwright, himself a seasoned escaper from the First World War, arranged food, shelter, companionship and a clothing allowance; he was tickled to have charge of a couple of wild colonials, strictly incognito, to enliven his social calendar.

Henry Cartwright would be one of the first to learn about Miles's death, and to subsequently list him, as he is still officially listed today, 'Died on Active Service'. In a sense, although Miles died in Spain, this is a true statement. In the words of Lord Templewood, 'he sacrificed his life for his country'.

There is nothing surprising about soldiers who saw service in the First World War cracking up in the Second. Chris Pugsley, in *A Bloody Road Home*, gives several examples of Great War veterans revelling at being once again in the front line in Greece in 1941, then, worn down by periods of prolonged strain, falling victim to mental and physical collapse. Nor does it take two wars to reach breaking point. Tubby Clayton, founder of Toc H, the soldiers' rest house in Flanders, tells of a captain with a Military Cross who first thought of the Great War as 'a rough and amusing football match'. Later in the war the captain refused to go back to France, and in 1920 entered a mental hospital in Putney. Studies show that Kiwis blooded at Gallipoli and on the Western Front told their comrades that they had reached the limit of endurance and couldn't take any more, effectively making a conscious decision to die in battle by seeking the bullet which has their name on it. In Flanders, a big curly-headed sergeant with an open smile was so imperturbable on patrol that men liked to go out with him. He didn't seem to notice the bullets or any of the sounds that set men's minds working to their undoing. One morning at Vimy, he stopped beside a crater to watch German mortar rounds being lobbed over his head like cricket balls. He became fascinated. His eyes glued to the live objects coming over, he began to ponder how long he had been in the battalion and muse about his own fate and inevitable demise by trench mortar. A fortnight later he reported sick to his medical officer and was sent away. He had gone mad.

As we have seen, Miles wore a mask. With it in place, certainly in the eyes of his men, he is surrounded by an aura that seems impenetrable and impossible to put into words.

The fascination in studying the motives of a man who destroys himself on the brink of freedom, after striving for it for the past two years, lies in trying to decide what is reality and what is illusion. In the end you conclude it is probably a mixture of both.

In the desert he wants to save his men, but when he can't he decides to go with them. Imprisoned in Italy he tells us that, like Scott of the Antarctic, he feels destined to fulfil some purpose in life, 'which I restlessly and blindly seek'. But really what he wants, you feel, is to be reunited with his wife in England. ('May it be soon!') In the next breath he asks her to send him 'a second set of summer-weight pyjamas, a couple of pairs of khaki shorts [he provides his waist measurement] and a few more handkerchiefs', sounding as normal and self-absorbed as the rest of us.

Oh, and he'd like a book to read, he says.

Small note. Miles the bookworm.

Miles is an avid reader. He is drawn to biographies of adventurers and explorers in the Heroic Age of Antarctic Exploration — Scott, Shackleton, Amundsen, Wilson; the last-named, Edward Wilson, Captain Scott's forgotten zoologist and artist on the ill-fated *Discovery* expedition, 'a character so near the divine as to be unapproachable by we ordinary mortals'. He is gripped by Dr Wilson's fortitude in George Seaver's account. Then Shackleton, the man whose story is one of history's greatest epics of survival. You would think that Shackleton's gift for leadership, inspiring the tenacious loyalty of his men trapped on the ice for nearly two years, would suggest an ideal role model. Yet it is the incompetent Scott, whose last journey is an epic of failure, whom Miles worships. He responds to Scott's weaknesses, to his great suffering, and he responds when the end comes in a raging blizzard to Scott's last words: '*We shall die like gentlemen … Our dead bodies must tell the tale.*'

And you wonder about his fascination and obsession with doomed men.

The night before he dies, Miles writes a farewell letter to his wife. He tells her he has been a failure and behaved dishonourably. The words 'failure' and 'dishonour' occur nine times in the first paragraph. The letter so impressed Viscount Templewood — Samuel Hoare, Britain's ambassador in Madrid when Miles reached Spain in 1943 — that at the end of the war he made it public. He quoted from the letter in a debate in the House of Lords.

Templewood attributed Miles's act to a mistaken belief that he had betrayed his country. 'He was a very gallant officer, with a magnificent military record. He wrote a letter to his wife saying his life was a failure and that he had committed the unforgivable sin of betraying his companions. There was not a word of truth in any of those suspicions: he was suffering from an illusion.'

The diarist Denton Welch said, after observing a group of young soldiers in wartime who were undressing behind lorries, 'laughing and swearing and shouting extravagantly', that he finally understood what was meant by the tradition of the army. It was something that 'exaggerated or completely changed the ordinary behaviour of ordinary civilian men'.

In Switzerland the days of waiting have turned into weeks, then months. At first Miles seems deliriously happy. He is living the life of Riley. He loafs about, goes shopping, goes to the dentist and has his teeth polished. He accepts invitations to tea, to dinner. Plays bridge until the small hours. Gads about in the markets, goes to Holy Communion, goes to the opera, goes sailing. Also dancing.

'Pleasant evening,' he tells his diary on 10 April 1943. 'I danced in my bedroom slippers.'

That summer he was one of the guests at a select wedding dinner at Neuhaus. Sitting almost opposite him was a psychoanalyst from Zurich, named Jung.

The only snag is the splinter of metal in his back, which is painful, and the chore of having to report regularly to the Swiss police. Hargest tells him to cheer up, and shows him a cable that has come from the high commission in London. It says, 'various things being done not to attempt anything on your own'.

He grows restless. Goes up into the Bernese Oberland, to Wengen and the Jungfrau, over to Zürich and Basle. He takes a tram and walks 'over the ridge to Boll. Lunch at the inn, then walked to Worb. Walked to wooded hill a mile behind Boll. Weeded flower garden when I got back.'

Hargest falls ill. Hargest has an old hip wound and spends most of the summer in hospital with a fever. Miles pampers and tends him like a son. He carps a bit. Here's Jim (he says) feeling sorry for himself, worrying about his prospects back in New Zealand after the war. Yet he's got a prosperous farm to go back to and an assured political future — while me: I face possible loss of employment and no prospects at all. 'Why should *he* worry?'

One day Miles hears Carton de Wiart speaking on the wireless. Memories of the escape from Vincigliata flood back. He writes to Philip Neame, saying he is stuck in Switzerland for the duration. He'd rather be back in prison in Italy, you feel, than 'safely here doing nothing while our country is fighting for its life'. Still, it must give a man a certain confidence to know, as he's heard on the grapevine, that he had momentarily been Freyberg's preferred choice to command the Division.

Hargest reminds him that Italy has capitulated and to get fit, man. *Stop bleating. Don't be so pessimistic. We'll get out sooner or later.*

He walks. He walks like blazes. He seems to be screwing himself up for some great feat. One day he walks 14 miles.

He goes rock climbing. He climbs up the Col de Jaman to the crest, easy going, but then confronted by 20 yards of razor edge, he funks it. He backs off, frightened.

You can see what is happening. Four years earlier in New Zealand, going for the top artillery job, he tells his diary he is 'bound to fail' (knowing that he won't). Now we have, '*Bugger you. I'll not fail*' (afraid that he will).

O, happy Switzerland!

There seems to be no way of getting out. And anyway, he says, 'Shall we be of any use when we do get out?'

Is that what he sees when he looks in the mirror? The spectre of Freyberg turning away? Of an army that's discarded him? The army appeals to almost every quality in him. It colours his mind and enters his dreams. Life is a campaign in which the army has become synonymous with life itself, demanding duty everlasting — duty to himself, to his country, to his name. It's his name that matters.

In the farewell letter to his wife, he tells her the army will not only sentence him to court martial but 'to death'. It will be merciless.

He reminds me of the DC10 pilot who speaks from beyond the grave in the Erebus episode, Jim Collins. Captain Collins was blamed by Air New Zealand for causing the crash on Mount Erebus in 1979, with the loss of 257 lives. Before he died, Collins told his wife, 'I know if I put so much as a scratch on one of their planes, they will be merciless towards me.'

* * *

But suddenly Miles is out of Purgatory, and off.

He has been to Winterthur with Cartwright for the day, helping settle parties of British POWs arriving from Italy into camps. 'Party of 58 arrived from Brigues at 2.30 p.m., very poorly clad,' his diary says. Then abruptly it breaks off.

Miles's Swiss diary begins with his arrival from Italy at the beginning of April 1943 and stops suddenly six months later on 6 October. There is little indication of what has been going on behind the scenes. What has happened is that the combined efforts of the New Zealand Government and British intelligence, the MI9, which is responsible for escape and evasion, have finally begun to bear fruit. Henry Cartwright in Bern has been contacted by the French underground. A courier has arrived in Geneva with instructions to guide 'two New Zealand generals' across France and on to England. Miles to go first.

Hargest writes: 'I was over at Lucerne when Miles rang up to say he was off, and to suggest that I should follow him later.'

The morning before he left, Miles called on the air attaché at the British Legation in Bern, Air Commodore Freddie West, VC, to say goodbye. The two had become friends.

Reg, as Freddie West would recall later, was a lovable individual, sensitive, 'and perhaps a little shy'. On this morning, West said, he seemed anxious. He talked about the responsibility he would be carrying across France and into Spain 'in not letting down the men and women who would be risking their lives to get him to freedom'.

Miles gave West a package — a wad of papers in an envelope — saying, 'If I don't make it, Freddie, or anything happens to me, will you please burn this and everything inside it.'

Hargest, however, writing a week or two later, appears to contradict West. He says that when he learned of Reg's death, 'I went over several letters Reg had left us to post to friends, and they were all *most* cheerful & full of hope & even gladness.'

The first indication that anything was wrong came about eight days later, on 21 October. It came from America. A wireless operator in Washington DC intercepted a shortwave radio message beamed to Europe from Sweden; it said that Stockholm radio had received word 'that a New Zealand general named Reginald Miller had committed suicide at Segarez in Spain where he was interned'. The news was cabled to Wellington by the New Zealand *chargé d'affaires* in Washington, Geoffrey Cox; it reached the government in Wellington on 22 October, and was copied to the high commission in London.

Reginald Miller?

A game of hunt the body began.

Wellington to Washington: *We know of no senior New Zealand officer at present interned in Spain ...*

Wellington to London: *There are persistent press reports that a Brigadier General Reg Miller has hanged himself in northern Spain. Please make immediate investigation ...*

Washington to Wellington: *Is this perhaps Brigadier Miles?*

Wellington to Washington: *To the best of our knowledge Miles is still in Switzerland.*

London to Wellington: *Circumstantially possible but have no positive information. Will investigate and inform earliest.*

In London, the War Office was called in. Brigadier Parks, the military liaison officer at the New Zealand High

Commission, tried to reach General Freyberg with the New Zealand Division — no easy task, for the Division was then in limbo, no fixed address, skirmishing somewhere on the River Sangro near the Adriatic in southern Italy. Eventually 'Brigadier Miller' was identified as 'Brigadier Miles' and the place of death 'Segarez' established as 'Figueras' in northern Spain. Meanwhile, insofar as he was able, the British consul in Barcelona was trying to fit together the pieces of a puzzle which had begun on 16 October 1943 with the arrival of Miles at a frontier village on the Spanish border named Puicerdà, to the north-west of Barcelona. Puicerdà was a fifty-minute train ride away.

'I have arrived safely,' Miles wrote to the consul in Barcelona, 'and am now at this frontier village. Have tried to get a taxi but it is apparently impossible so I must take the train and presumably be picked up by the police. I have an emergency passport to prove my identity; and trust you will not leave me too long in durance vile.'

That was 16 October. The letter arrived in Barcelona on 17 October.

From Barcelona the news was passed to the ambassador in Madrid, Samuel Hoare. In Barcelona the consul, seemingly unconcerned, sat back and waited on further news. Three days later it came. Miles, writing again on 19 October, said he had been apprehended by the police on the frontier, but was now 'on parole' in a hotel just north of Barcelona, in the town of Figueras. He was physically very well and had enough money for his immediate needs.

Miles added, 'The Chief of Police tells me he will write to you in a few days; but I do not wish you to advise my wife or friends that I am in Spain until I know whether I am to proceed to England or Egypt.' (Georgie was living in London, packing war prisoners' parcels for the Merchant Navy.)

Two days later, on 21 October, the consul was telephoned by the civil governor, who said that Miles had committed suicide. He had been found hanging in his hotel bedroom.

At this point the consul, David Francis, is moved to act. He instigates an inquiry. The inquiry reveals that around 3am on 20 October, the day after he reached the hotel, Miles appeared to have climbed from the patio giving off his room and onto the roof, intending to throw himself down into the street; he slipped and fell, breaking a flower pot; he had then gone into the bedroom and hung himself from a water pipe in the ceiling, using the cord from the sunblind of his window.

The water pipes had been torn away from their sockets and had burst, flooding the room and the floor below.

An autopsy had been held, and a priest persuaded to overcome his religious scruples and conduct a funeral service. The autopsy report read in part:

> *External appearance of the body, that of a man of ordinary stature, perhaps rather tall, corpulent, well developed and of good physique ... He is dressed in greenish grey pyjamas with red and green stripes.*
>
> *On removal of the pyjamas, not the slightest sign of external violence or struggle is observed ...*
>
> *CONCLUSIONS*
>
> *1. Death was due to asphyxia ...*
>
> *2. Since there is no sign of external violence the opinion is that it is clearly a case of suicide ...*

In New Zealand, the government learned that Miles had been buried by the Spanish authorities with full military honours; that he had written a letter proving he intended to kill himself; and that he had done so while of unsound mind, of which there was no doubt. (This all according to Brigadier Park at the high commission in London.) At which point the word 'doubt' enters the script, and the clouds its negation are intended to dispel begin to gather.

'The strange thing is,' Hargest says in a letter written from Madrid the following month, 'that he had written to people here just a few hours before and was quite cheerful ... He was evidently much worried about me as he left a scribbled note on a newspaper, "Very worried about Jim, please try & contact Henry [Cartwright, the military attaché]." And also he imagined that sometime, somewhere he had talked too much.'

According to Georgie Miles, no one at the high commission in London had seen the contents of her husband's letter. She had received it under seal, after it had been authenticated by the British, and kept it to herself. Some days earlier, she says, she had had a premonition. She had called on the New Zealand high commissioner, Bill Jordan, and begged him to allow her to go to Switzerland to be with her husband. Bill Jordan, she says, was embarrassed.

'As I was leaving, he said to me, "We are expecting him here soon. Keep it to yourself."'

Georgie kept the letter, written on the day before he died, and showed it to no one. It was a farewell letter, addressed: *'To My Wife'*. It has not been published before. It begins:

> *My Darling,*
> *This is the end of nearly two years of plotting, planning, working, striving, to get back to you and to my duty with our army. Three days ago I was walking happily down a road in Northern Spain, with freedom, honour, love and duty, all within my grasp. Yet within a few hours I had failed miserably, stupidly, dishonourably, and as time goes on my failure and dishonour increases. As I cannot silence my wagging tongue any other way I must take this one. My failure, apart from its consequences for others, involved for me court-martial and inevitable sentence of death. This the New Zealand Government might not confirm; and you would be tied for the rest of your life to a dishonoured living corpse. Far better that I should be dead and you free. I have loved you constantly and devotedly, dear, and have longed to get back to you. But now you must try to forget the name I have dishonoured ...*

It ends:

> *Beloved wife, daughters, brothers and sisters, friends: good-bye to you all.*
> *REGINALD MILES*

This is the letter that will be cited in the House of Lords by Samuel Hoare (Lord Templewood) at the end of the war. There is the clear implication that Miles, under interrogation, thought he had betrayed his friends and compromised the underground escape network; that he had done wrong and that he blamed himself.

It soon became evident that he had not betrayed anyone. Proof of this was the safe arrival in Spain of Hargest a few days later. James Hargest was smuggled through occupied France to the Spanish border by the same underground courier who a few days earlier had accompanied Miles, and by exactly the same route. (Hargest subsequently reached England via Gibraltar.)[2]

None of this rules out the possibility that Miles, after reaching Figueras, was put into a cell and subjected to the

2 Hargest died in Normandy during the 1944 D-Day invasion. He landed with the 50th Northumbrian Division in June 1944, attached as an observer; he was killed by mortar fire during the assault on Caen.

sort of interrogation or given a drug that did tip the balance of his mind. This is what Georgie believed. The tone of Miles's last two letters of 19 October — one written in the morning, the other, the farewell letter, later in the day, presumably in the evening — is, as she says, very different.

The first letter does not appear to have been written by someone 'suffering from an illusion'. Georgie believed her husband was 'got at'. So did his guide, Gabriel Nahas, who was nineteen at the time. Nahas worked for the French resistance under the *nom de guerre* Georges Brantès. After the war he was decorated by France and the United States, where he achieved a name as a medical researcher, campaigning against drug abuse. When I met him in New Zealand, he was still wearing on his wrist the watch Hargest gave him when they set out on their journey across France.

'I was astonished when I learned Miles was dead,' Nahas said. 'Nobody in Figueras believed it was suicide. When I left him at the border he was fit and well. Everything had gone according to plan.' The suicide story, he said to me, was not credible.

Nahas believed Miles was interrogated by Spanish agents working for the Gestapo. It sounds feasible. Other theories — accounts published in English newspapers, claiming he was carrying coded messages or clandestine documents subsequently reported 'missing' from his belongings — are less so. As to the wad of papers he left with Freddie West, telling him to burn them if anything happened: what did West do? He burned them. Without, he said, even opening the package.

Our best witness is Georgie. She was twelve years younger than her husband. What do we know about her? She was very English, very level-headed, and very determined. In 1943, Georgie Miles began bombarding the War Office, MI9 and other authorities with questions. Soon she had an answer to at least one question. It concerned the Spanish authorities in Figueras: namely, that that part of northern Spain was bristling with enemy agents, and that the governor of Figueras prison, one Señor Mena, and the chief of police, were ardent Nazi sympathisers. Forty years later, she was still at it.

'I too was caught by the Spanish police and sent to Figueras,' a member of the European Parliament, James Scott-Hopkins, wrote to her in 1982. 'It was a rotten prison. I fear anything could have happened there.'

Why was he in Figueras? What was her husband doing in Figueras when he wished to go to Barcelona? Georgie wanted to know. Oh, and why did the postmortem by Spanish doctors, which said he had no distinguishing marks but only war wounds, fail to mention the large birthmark on his right thigh? And his toiletries? 'When they were handed to me in his briefcase, I found that the shaving soap, toothpaste, tablets, etc. had all been cut to shreds.' And so on.

We shall have to leave it there. 'After all' — a final sally from Georgie — 'his letter to me does say: "Three days ago I was walking happily down a road in Northern Spain." It is what happened to my husband in those three days that I want to find out.'

The answer, I suspect, is that we shall never know.

Perhaps Hargest got it right. Among the countless studies available to us today of soldiers in both wars who cracked — or didn't crack — after being slowly worn down in conditions of prolonged stress, Miles is a peculiarity. He doesn't seem to fit anywhere. Strangely, those who survived best and were the least affected were the highly neurotic and the schizoids. What in peacetime had been a defect or handicap proved of benefit in war. These were men outside the group. In many ways Miles, too, was outside the group. But in Spain he was without the one thing that might have helped: human contact. He was alone, detached from responsibility and deprived of companionship, as Hargest says, for the first time in his life.

'There could be no question,' Hargest wrote, 'of force anywhere & I think he just broke down in the night and went straight into his action. Poor Reg.'

* * *

You need a ladder to visit the grave in Figueras. The coastal town of Figueras (population 45,000), 30 kilometres from the French border at the foot of the Pyrénées, is the birthplace of the Spanish surrealist painter Salvador Dali. We can imagine little Salvador — well, almost — going paddling with bucket and spade on the beach directly below the Hôtel Gran Paris, where Reg Miles was discovered dead in 1943. Today the Hôtel Gran Paris is a toy factory. But the celebrated museum designed by Salvador Dali, which is one of the attractions of the town, is still there, largely unchanged.

You will need a ladder, as Miles's grandson Bill Dawson and his wife, Marilyn, discovered when they visited the cemetery, because the grave is a niche in a wall four levels high above ground. '*Niche no 894, piso 4, Figueras Municipal Cemetery.*'

Bill found a ladder, climbed up and read the inscription on the tablet:

Brigadier Reginald Miles
(6191)
C.B.E., D.S.O. & BAR, M.C.
N.Z. ARTILLERY
20 October 1943. Age 50

The cemetery itself is by the old bull ring, he tells us. It resembles a vast wine rack almost a hundred metres long. Reg's niche is one among scores of identical metal drawers let into the walls like filing cabinets. Over 9 feet up, it is a lonely resting place for one of New Zealand's most decorated soldiers: the man who took the Second Divisional Artillery overseas, trained it in England, led it in Greece and rebuilt it in North Africa — in short, the Father of the Divisional Artillery.

I'm not sure about this last bit. Miles's legacy is disputed. I haven't mentioned it before. It needed a ladder, I suppose, to jog my memory.

* * *

As with the grave, so with a citadel called Quesnoy. A hundred years ago you needed a ladder to scale the ramparts and conquer the medieval town of Le Quesnoy in northern France. Le Quesnoy is one of those towns that recur in history. It had been occupied by the Germans since the start of the Great War in 1914, and was freed by New Zealand troops a week before the war ended in 1918.

The fortress of Quesnoy is where in 1336 British soldiers first tasted cannon fire. In 1918, nearly 600 years later, the same citadel was barring the way through Belgium to Germany. Miles, then a major, had rejoined his battery in France from England, and was given the job of planning the artillery attack. It is now that we learn about 'the creeping barrage'. This was an innovation to protect attacking troops by curtains of fire exploding in timed 'lifts' — a delicate business, because if the shells exploded too near the front of the advancing infantry, the troops risked being killed by 'friendly fire', and if too far back it left them exposed to destruction by the enemy lying in wait. Miles, we read, worked on the battle plans uninterruptedly for two days and nights.

When the attack went in, the horse-drawn guns — leap-frogging battery by battery over intermediate distances along a 5-mile front — protected the infantry by heavy barrages and machine-gun fire all the way. It took the best part of a day. It worked. It worked so well that, at the end when they scaled the walls, the defence inside collapsed. A sudden rush carried a 60-foot wall, enabling it to be scaled by ladders and the breach widened. Thousands of German prisoners were taken. The civilians, in the words of Spud Murphy, garlanded the New Zealanders with flowers, 'delirious with joy'. Not one shell had fallen inside the town.

It was the last major battle on the Western Front and, for Miles, a signal contribution to his legacy and symbolic nickname, 'Father of the family'. But wait. There are rival contenders.

The original father of the artillery was an avuncular character named Parkinson, another Duntroon graduate. In 1919, however, Parkinson foolishly diverted regimental funds to pay for a new roof on his house and was stood down. His misdemeanour paved the way for Miles. Then at the end of 1941, when Miles was captured, in came Weir. Steve Weir is the man who is usually credited for inventing 'stonk' and 'murder' — gunner parlance for new techniques of fire developed originally by Miles rehearsing with the infantry in Syria; and then, refined by Weir, adopted and championed by the British Eighth Army at the time of Alamein and afterwards. Weir was Miles's protégé and natural successor. After Miles was captured, he led the artillery across North Africa and through the Italian campaign, and has a strong claim to 'godfather' status. Well, sure. He lived longer and achieved more. But Weir's record is also spotted.

At the end of the war, Steve Weir was promoted general and placed in command of a British division in southern Austria. There, he was involved in an incident in which thousands of Russian Cossacks, having laid down their arms and surrendered in the expectation of being treated humanely, were forcibly repatriated to the Soviet Union to face almost certain imprisonment or death. Some had fought for the Germans; most had fled Russia after the revolution and were no longer Soviet citizens. It was an ugly incident, casting Weir in a bad light.

So. Weir? Or Miles?

Weir was the younger man. He was knighted in 1960. Montgomery considered him a master gunner and 'one of the great artillery men in history'. Steve Weir was thrusting and over six feet tall. But with his nuggety frame he looked smaller. Reg Miles, the gentle giant, was less tall, under six feet, yet he seemed somehow bigger. Weir was less broody than the unpredictable Miles — 'Mad Miles', somebody once called him. Nobody, according to Spud Murphy, would have said that about Steve Weir.

In his history of the New Zealand Artillery, Murphy, describing the capture of Miles in the desert, writes:

> *Reggie Miles was an all-round gunner, interested and accomplished in every sphere of gunnery; but he was more than that. And when he disappeared, into the swirling smoke and dust at Belhamed in the company of some of his beloved gunners, it was as if the Divisional Artillery had lost its father.*

Somehow, to this writer at least, despite the brooding and the irascibility, that is the image that endures above everything else.

PETER MAHON

I never met Peter Mahon, the late Mr Justice Mahon QC, of the Erebus inquiry. I am not sure I would have liked him. I suspect I would have been in awe somewhat of his tongue, at least. When I met the family, his widow, Margarita Mahon, told me that it was usually his tongue that got him into trouble. His son, Sam, by way of variation, said it was more his great learning and irreverence that occasioned jealousy and upset some of his colleagues — adding that, as a bit of a wit, his father sometimes turned it upon himself.

Sam Mahon tells the story of a family Christmas in Auckland during which, as they sat around the table in their party hats eating dinner, five of them — father, mother, Sam, his younger brother Tim and his sister, Janet — his father took out a thin cigar and lit it. 'Father, it isn't polite to smoke between courses,' Janet chided. Whereupon Judge Mahon blew out a stream of smoke towards the ceiling, rested the cigar on a plate and skipped nimbly around the table, tapping his wife and daughter lightly on the breast as he passed, then sat down and picked up his cigar where he had left it. 'Gracious, Peter, what on earth was that about?' said Margarita, mystified, as they all were. 'That? That, Mother,' the judge said, after a pause, 'was the titter that ran around the crowd.'

At the time, Peter Mahon was a High Court judge of some standing. He was quite different from other judges, though. An erratic sleeper, he rose early to work on his judgments, moulding language as a poet does — poetry and the English language being a great love, second only to the law. He was never happier, his son says, than when he was sitting down with a glass of malt in one hand and a volume of poetry in the other. He read Gibbon and Macaulay, but he also went to war in Italy, where he was introduced to Dante. He quoted Dante in the original Italian, and would have agreed with Auden that poetry is not concerned so much with, or not only with, communicating feelings, as it is with extending our knowledge of good and evil.

And so he chose an iambic pentameter such as Shakespeare might have used to coin the phrase 'an orchestrated litany of lies', in the wake of the Erebus disaster. It was his way of exposing a cover-up by Air New Zealand and its collusion with the Ministry of Civil Aviation, whose incompetence he said had caused the tragedy. The phrase would ultimately prove his undoing. But he felt for those who had died and he wanted a phrase that would stick.

This, then, is the story of that phrase, which would enter the national consciousness and become one of the most famous expressions in aviation legal history. It symbolises and celebrates a man's standing in the wider world, but it also acts as a shibboleth, a codeword or test of something darker in a small society. It speaks of a man tilting at windmills in a judicial village. Of a champion of dissent who is edged out and crushed by a small-minded Establishment. It speaks also of a hidden animosity between two eminent practitioners of the law, one of whom would end up with, at the hands of the other, his reputation in tatters.

Just to remind ourselves: Peter Mahon was appointed by the government as a sole Royal Commissioner to investigate the loss of an Air New Zealand DC10 airliner which crashed on the slopes of Mount Erebus in the Antarctic, killing all 257 people on board. It was the fourth-worst air disaster in history. The date, 28 November 1979. The Commissioner's brief was to inquire into the cause of the crash, and report his findings. What was unusual was the absence of a tribunal or committee: with only a small ancillary staff and two counsel to help him, Mahon alone was to hear the evidence, sift through it and report. It was, in the circumstances, a surprising appointment.

Mahon had always been on the outside, a man of discernment and mercurial wit who could be relied on — he was a prince of raconteurs — to draw a small crowd at most gatherings. He was not a family man, but one much admired and loved. He grew up in Canterbury in modest circumstances. His father was an accountant, a cantankerous but principled Roman Catholic who allowed his daughters — Peter's two sisters — the freedom to renounce Catholicism and join the Church of England, but not the son. Leniency, love towards the only son was denied. 'A sense of "being different", Peter's daughter Janet says, 'was always there'. Similarly at his Catholic boarding school, St Bede's, he came top in all the exams but was not allowed to become dux. After all, he was a mere scholarship boy.

It is popularly supposed that judges are unworldly beings who have benefited from privilege and are unused to sullying their hands (and bibs) in the kitchens and sinkholes of life. Peter Mahon was not one of these. A glance at his war file is instructive. He had left school in 1940 at 17 and begun a law degree, volunteering for the war which would interrupt his studies by fiddling his age, according to his widow Margarita. He didn't, as it happened, get away until 1943. Upon enlisting, he was asked the following questions:

Age on leaving school? *17*

Did you pass Matriculation? *Yes*

Can you drive a car and lorry? *Yes*

Can you ride a motor-cycle? *Yes*

Can you ride a horse? *Yes*

What are your hobbies? *Shooting*

Sam Mahon, in a memoir, gives us the shape of the father — grey coat and hat, briefcase, a perpetual cigarette in his mouth, a twinkle in the eye. He explores his father's duality, the intimate observer of Nature who delighted in pointing out to his small son the difference between a chaffinch and a warbler, as he delighted equally in catching snakes and shooting animals in the wild — a paradox matched by Mahon's eyes, which to some were blue and others, marigold brown. The army recorded his eyes as both blue and brown, but found him an expert marksman.

Posted to Italy at or about the time of Cassino, Mahon became a despatch rider, then a sniper. Shortly before he died, Mahon wrote a short story in which he describes a winter with his battalion bogged down in the plains of Lombardy. He is in the front line on the banks of the Senio, near Faenza. In the story, evidently autobiographical and entitled 'The Sniper', he captures the moment when he picked off his first enemy German.

He was staring through the mist at a gap in a stopbank. Two figures appeared, vague blurs in the middle distance, then vanished. They flickered in and out of view. He put down the binoculars, rested his eyes and took them up again. One figure had returned He expelled the air from his lungs and took the first pressure, then when the walking figure neared the intersection of the crossed hairs of the telescope, he squeezed the trigger. He slammed the bolt forward and reloaded. He picked up the gun again. Only one figure was in sight — he was kneeling on the ground and supporting himself on his arms. 'Jesus,' he thought. 'I've got him.'

Italy was seminal for Mahon, and not just because of the war. Buttoned up in a heavy overcoat, wearing woollen mittens and a balaclava with a gap for the eyes, he passes long hours staring through binoculars across a field of vision hemmed in by the Senio and by ditches booby-trapped with Shu and S mines. Off-duty, he studies papers in criminal law and contracts for his Bar exams and plays Crown and Anchor and Poker with the boys.

There was a larrikin side. 'Cut it out, Bill,' he tells a platoon mate for wasting time dicing the pack between his fingers. 'You'll shuffle the tits off the queen.' He is speaking here not as an officer but as an NCO, a lance corporal or corporal, not commissioned. Serving with the ranks and mixing with them, he even sounds like them. Easy to see where he got the rapier cut and thrust to his tongue, giving him later that vernacular edge which would become so distinctive and set him apart from other judges.

(He was commissioned in the field and spent the end of the war in Tokyo. There is a family story that his field promotion was the result of gallantry — an act for which he was rewarded by the offer of a medal or a commission. Mahon chose the commission, so the story goes; but this, like so many incidents omitted from battalion histories, is hard to verify.)

He was a tall young man, lantern-jawed, with a long, thin, finely drawn face, deceptively stern. His son describes a man hard to get to know, a man of volatile clarity of thought who was 'constantly changing trains' (a nice foretaste of his coming leap into a Royal Commissioner's carriage); and of his sense of mischief and absurdity, the *enfant terrible* to come.

However, when he returned from the war Peter Mahon's unorthodoxy was not immediately apparent. In Christchurch he entered the Crown Law Office. He had gone away a private and returned a second lieutenant, completing his studies and being admitted to the Bar in 1947.

He spent some years working under the Crown Solicitor, Arthur Donnelly, and then at the age of 34, after the latter died unexpectedly, he inherited the post himself. For a young man working his way up it was a good inside job, with no 'heavy lifting' and with prospects — a comfortable future — assured until retirement. Yet within five years Mahon had resigned as Crown Solicitor and set up as an independent barrister.

It was a risky step. Christchurch in the 1950s was not a litigation city. With most of the legal workload divided between three or four firms, if a client wanted to litigate, they would usually be pointed to a journeyman-barrister operating outside the firm. That way, there was no risk of losing the client. Mahon broke the mould: he was the first barrister sole in town, the first to go independent on his own. He established himself in a former dress shop. When he immediately got work and then became successful, he was both admired for his skill and resented as a turncoat.

His style soon showed. His skill lay in being able to cut through argument and humbug to expose a key issue, and he had an ability to analyse a mass of complex issues to support his conclusions. To relieve the boredom in court he would sometimes amuse himself by writing notes to his (female) associate and pass them to her when she needed to keep a straight face. There was also a flair for public pronouncements, as when he spoke out about the wisdom of clients taking their tax problems to accountants, who would, he said, be inclined to cosy up to the Inland Revenue Department rather than do battle for their clients. To protests from the Society of Accountants, Mahon replied that he was reminded of the Russian who was sentenced to 25 years for calling Premier Krushchev a fool — 'five years for insulting the premier and 20 for giving away a state secret' — recounts Glyn Strange in *Brief Encounters*. So far, so unorthodox. Mahon was rapidly promoted.

What is interesting is that in such a tiny profession where cronyism prevailed — there were scarcely a dozen independent barristers in the whole country — he worked his way up entirely without connections. Queen's Counsels (QCs) were rare. Awareness of the snobberies of Bar and

Bench probably acted as a spur to his native ambitions. By the time he took silk and became a Queen's Counsel, he had an unusual depth and range of experience — he knew criminal law and commercial law backwards (few lawyers did both) — and was acting for clients all over the country. He was made a QC in 1971, and the same year appointed a Supreme Court judge in Auckland. (At that time, what we now know as the High Court was called the Supreme Court.) His promotion was said to be so rapid that while serving on the judicial circuit out of Auckland, he was still attempting to clear up work from his Christchurch office.

Slow of speech and hesitant — but it was a studied hesitancy — he would approach a case with little apparent preparation, then stand and deliver fluently without notes. While not a great advocate, he was a skilled presenter, with a feeling for the evidence. He had something of a seer's ability to divine the thoughts and motivation of witnesses. His judgments were lucid if wordy (a mix of charm, vanity, and love of language); and his sentencing often peculiar — severe and harsh on young criminals and rapists, he was oddly lenient towards drink-drivers and racehorse owners where dope was involved. It was a small world then, the Bar and Bench, with only 16 Supreme Court judges plus the Chief Justice in the entire country. The courts were dominated by a vigorous oral tradition and the personality of the jury advocates, who all knew one another; it was a life more leisurely and a profession still to be enjoyed, with gatherings over drinks and coffee, barbs and lampoons part of the culture, gossip created which might scar a jurist's conceit but not destroy his reputation.

Mahon stood out because he had an ego. He also had a view on the proper role of a judge — call it the Mahon Factor. It had to do with charity in its purest sense, or, to use another old-fashioned word, mercy. It is exemplified by the case of a gentleman named Tindall, who attempted to sue the Crown after being convicted, unjustifiably he said, of speeding. The case came before Justice Mahon who dismissed it. Tindall bowed, left the court, and returned half an hour later with a quantity of tomatoes which he aimed and hurled at the judge. One hit Peter Mahon on the bib. He was covered in tomato. A lawyer who was an eyewitness notes that Mahon simply took a handkerchief and wiped himself down before adjourning for lunch, then he organised for lunch to be sent down to his assailant, who had been restrained and taken to the cells. After lunch he called Tindall to his chambers and talked to him, then sent him on his way.

According to the witness, 'Peter knew as well as anybody the man was obsessed with his case. He was lucky.

He could easily have been done for contempt.' Clearly Mahon, however, felt that following the letter of the law in this instance was disproportionate to the crime, which merely reflected the man's distorted balance.

In a heyday of judge 'personalities' (Barrowclough, Wild, North, Cooke, Speight), Mahon, who liked to call himself a reactionary, was far from eccentric. His judgments were challenged and sometimes overturned on questions of probity like any else's, but they were not ridiculed or derided for their tone as well. That is, at least not until another returned serviceman and Supreme Court judge, slightly higher in the pecking order, named Woodhouse, was elevated to the Court of Appeal in 1974.

I could at this point, in the run-up to Erebus, enlist your sympathy by citing a number of cases illustrating the Mahon Factor. (A case about two speculating vicars comes to mind; also a judgment involving a mouse in a milk bottle which was subsequently adapted for the stage.) But I prefer to keep it short and allow a fragment to speak for the whole.

The fragment is the Parker–Hulme case (Christchurch, 1954), the sensational trial at which Pauline Parker and Juliet Hulme were convicted of murdering Pauline Parker's mother by smashing her head with a brick wrapped inside a stocking. Peter Mahon, then 31, was acting for the Crown as junior to the Crown Prosecutor, Alan Brown. It was Alan Brown's first big case. He was a theatrical figure and a heavy drinker. Determined to win, he became overwrought towards the end of the trial, and broke down in tears. Brown was on the verge of mental collapse. (He was subsequently committed to Ashburn Hall, a private mental hospital, in Dunedin.) Mahon took over.

Peter Mahon's use of the vernacular, the *mot juste*, is evident already in Brown's opening address, in which he described the crime as a cold, premeditated act by 'two highly intelligent but precocious and dirty-minded little girls'. Such imagery, reverberating in the media, would enter the annals of crime literature. There is no proof that the phrase 'dirty-minded little girls' is Peter Mahon's. But it sounds like him. It seems to foreshadow another, even more graphic phrase designed to stick, that would follow nearly three decades later.

In the Parker-Hulme case the defence pleaded insanity. On the eve of the closing speeches, and before he was due to sum up, the presiding judge, Mr Justice Adams, called the defence and prosecuting counsel into chambers and said that he did not intend to put the defence of insanity to the jury. He would instead direct the jury to enter a verdict of guilty. The defence counsel protested that if that happened he would immediately appeal. Prosecutor Peter Mahon went further. He said to the judge that if he did not allow the insanity plea to go in, the prosecution would withdraw from the case. The judge relented.

Mahon was offended; his sense of fair play aroused. He had delivered an ultimatum which had stopped the judge from ruling to the advantage of the prosecution — that is, in Mahon's favour. The example is symbolic. It suggests to me a man of integrity who was nobody's lackey and who could not under any circumstances be bought. Why then, of all people — you may ask — did Prime Minister Muldoon appoint Mahon to the Erebus inquiry? It is a good question. The short answer is that the prime minister made a mistake.

* * *

So now we get to the point where a Royal Commission of Inquiry is about to be set up to look into the Erebus crash.

Now while Muldoon clearly did not know his man in selecting Mahon as Commissioner, to be fair, he was by this time in some difficulty. The effect of the Erebus crash on the country cannot be underestimated. In such a small country, the sheer number of deaths meant that it seemed everyone knew someone who was affected by the crash. It being a special flight, it also meant that a number of prominent persons were among those who had lost their lives or who had been bereaved.

A comprehensive report by the Chief Inspector of Air Accidents, Ron Chippendale, was imminent; it had been commissioned by the government within days of the crash. Its conclusion, though not yet made public, was rumoured to be pilot error — the plane had been flying too low in an area of bad visibility, the pilots unable to detect through the cloud the rising ground in front of them. Uncertain of their position, they had breached a basic altitude rule forbidding descent below 16,000 feet in their approach, which had inevitably led to tragedy. This made sense; the report's conclusions appeared sound. Why a second report? Well, there were further complications. Mr Muldoon, as Minister of Finance, was the chief shareholder in Air New Zealand, which was attracting allegations of a conflict of interest from some quarters. With his office full of model airplanes, it would also seem he had a personal interest in aviation. In the end, such was the scale of the tragedy and the clamour for a full-scale inquiry that Muldoon had no option but to acquiesce to public opinion and set up an independent, judicial inquiry.

But who to head the inquiry? He took advice from, among others, Des Dalgety and Lloyd Brown. Dalgety, a civil jurist and Mr Muldoon's personal lawyer, was deputy-chairman of the Air New Zealand board. Lloyd Brown QC, a leading Auckland barrister, had been named the airline's chief counsel. It should be quite straightforward, Muldoon was advised: it needed someone with a sharp mind, able to cut through complex issues and go straight for the nub without being sidetracked. It had worked before, on the Marginal Lands Board inquiry, and the Colin Moyle inquiry. The prime minister would have the answer he wanted.

There are several versions of what happened next. All for some reason involve lunch with the Danish Consul, a former cavalry officer with a difficult name. Erik Johan Støyer Kjaer's lunches at Princes Court in the heart of Auckland's professional club-land — with a routine of heel-clicking, bowing, fingertip-kissing and three or four beakers of Aquavit — were legendary. Lloyd Brown's chambers were also in Princes Court. He and Mahon were friends besides occasional guests at these lunches, where one day Mahon confided to Brown, when the subject of Erebus surfaced, that he wouldn't mind a change of scenery. After eight years on the Bench he was finding life a bit humdrum. In Wellington the prime minister, with no reliable commissioner in sight, was under pressure: months after the crash had occurred and public criticism of the delay in getting answers was mounting. He spoke to Dalgety again. Dalgety spoke to Brown, who said, well, as it happened he did know someone who might answer. Clever chap, quick-witted, who was finding life humdrum and looking for something a bit more challenging. A judge he knew, who was someone he could vouch for. And who was, besides, Brown said, 'a good conservative chap'.

Deal done. Mahon was appointed. Lloyd Brown and Peter Mahon were both high-fliers. Brown, a society lawyer, high-flying, mercurial, humorous. They were friends. They played golf together, and enjoyed — Mahon was an assiduous punter — the horses. They got on famously. Peter Mahon later told Greg McGee he believed that he was chosen so that Lloyd Brown would be able to exploit their relationship and keep an eye on him. Instead, the relationship would be wrecked, utterly. The prime minister, thinking he had found a pair of safe hands, was thus twice mistaken.

Mr Muldoon made a press statement. He explained why a sole commissioner was preferable to a committee or a tribunal, and how difficult it had been to find someone of integrity who was capable of mastering the technical details of a big commercial jet yet who had not previously been associated with Air New Zealand. He sounded satisfied with his choice, even pleased. Mr Justice Mahon may also have been initially pleased.

* * *

Nearly seven months had passed when hearings began in downtown Auckland in July 1980. Just a few days before this, the Chippendale Report had been made public. It concluded that the aircrew's fatal mistake had been to commence a descent below the authorised 16,000 feet, and, reading it, Mahon was inclined to agree. ('Report points to error by DC10 captain', 'Flight thousands of feet too low', the newspapers headlined.) Mahon read the chief inspector's report several times; Chippendale appeared to have covered every aspect of the occurrence; and the implications of the plane being off-course, lost in cloud and flying too low, thus sheeting home the blame to the pilots and clearing the airline, as paraphrased in the press, seemed 'quite correct'.

Nonetheless, some claimed that the report had been rushed through by the government in order to upstage and undermine the commissioner; others, that the technical data revealed by Chippendale, a former air force squadron leader, would be of great help to him. Either way, Mahon at the outset was not unduly disturbed; the inquiry appeared straightforward; he was concerned only, he says, by a story about a computer mistake — corroborated by Chippendale — that the plane's flight coordinates had been changed at the last moment.

The chief inspector agreed. In his report he had noted the error in the flight plan, but this, he said, had not misled the crew and had had no bearing on the cause of the accident. He criticised the Air New Zealand management for a number of breaches and errors, despite a claim by the chief executive, Mr Davis, that 'the navigation information and flight plan were accurate and entirely in order'. But these errors, Mr Chippendale said, had not caused the crash either.

The facts, as Mahon was about to discover, were slightly different.

Only minutes before the crash, passengers were taking photographs out of the windows. They did not know, as the pilots did not know, that just before they took off, someone at Air New Zealand had punched the wrong digits into the plane's navigational computer and omitted to tell the pilots of the late change. Nor did the passengers realise, as the pilots did not realise, that as a result they were 27 miles off-course. At the moment of impact they were flying in clear air, but because of a trick of polar light, known as 'whiteout', the mountain in front of them was invisible. Without any apprehension on the part of the pilots or anyone else on board, they flew straight into it.

This inconvenient truth was not immediately apparent.

* * *

These were public hearings on oath. Separate counsel appeared for Air New Zealand, for the estates of the two pilots who died, for the national pilots' association and for a consortium representing the estates of the dead passengers. Mahon himself spoke seldom. He listened. His suspicions were first aroused, he says, when at the outset the airline made no opening statement of its position. It adopted a wait-and-see attitude (admit nothing, say nothing) — 'as if it was being prosecuted in a court of law and was uncertain of the reliability of its evidence'. Witnesses appeared vague or secretive, sometimes hostile. One of the architects of sightseeing flights, the airline's chief pilot, Captain Gemmell, was evasive and treated questions by the Commission's chief counsel, David Baragwanath, with barely concealed contempt.

Mahon had expected to be shown a wealth of documentation, but found that the little the airline produced tended to favour its stance of pilot error, while documents found at the crash site which might have pointed in an opposite direction, such as the pages of a ring-bound notebook carried by the captain of the flight, Jim Collins, had unaccountably disappeared or been tampered with. Tapes had been doctored, a crucial four-minute section from the cockpit voice recorder had been erased, and the 'black box' read-out interfered with; it also appeared that a number of files had been declared 'surplus' and shredded by the airline on the orders of the chief executive.

As Mahon's suspicions grew, so did the obduracy of the airline's chief witnesses. The latter clung to pilot error, supporting Chippendale and blaming the pilots for breaking an inviolable rule and descending below 16,000 feet, or 4000 feet above the top of the mountain. The 'rule' was of course on paper only; it was a requirement by the civil aviation air ministry, and was regularly waived as a courtesy to Air New Zealand. In practice, the Antarctic flights were programmed to fly down the middle of McMurdo Sound, a flat expanse well clear of

Mount Erebus. Approaching the air traffic control base at McMurdo, the aircrews inquired of the base for permission to descend to 2000 feet and lower — which, cloud-cover permitting, was regularly granted. There was no danger: McMurdo Sound was flat, unrelieved by mountainous or rising terrain, with unlimited visibility for 40 miles. These were sightseeing flights after all.

Yet, when shown photographic evidence, widely advertised and published in Air New Zealand's own newspaper, witnesses at the hearings shook their heads and looked blank. They professed ignorance.

Mahon would say later that, had the airline been candid and disclosed the blunders it was attempting to cover up, it would have retained a measure of public respect and the inquiry would have been over in three or four weeks. Instead, it would last eight months.

For better or worse, Mahon's name today is associated in the profession with two words, 'natural justice' — for worse, because he is accused by his critics of bias, of being unfair to those witnesses he disbelieved, by not telling them so and giving them an opportunity to reply. He might have told a witness to his face, 'I don't believe you.' But that was not his job. He was there to listen, and to report. His problem, assuming he recognised it at the time, was how do you reconcile what you are hearing from mature and apparently responsible witnesses with the application of natural justice?

Two examples. The question is once again altitude.

On the stand is Captain Lawson, one of the Air New Zealand briefing pilots; he is being examined by David Baragwanath, senior counsel for the Commission:

> *Baragwanath:* So in your view then, the phrase 'as the DC10 cruised at 2000 feet past the Antarctic's Mt Erebus', properly translated, meant, 'as the DC10 cruised at 16,000 feet over the top of Mt Erebus?'
>
> *Captain Lawson:* I would have to assume that.

Second example, Morrie Davis. Morrison Ritchie Davis, the chief executive of Air Zealand, appears — rather than the outspoken abrasive individual of repute — 'subdued, highly cooperative and apprehensive'. He is one of the last in a line of senior witnesses, and his theme when cross-examined is, as with the others, that there was a minimum safe altitude of 16,000 feet which in no circumstances could be departed from. At which point, as Justice Mahon writes in *Verdict on Erebus*:

> *I asked him a few questions myself. One of my final questions was how the airline could have published one million copies of the* Travelling Times *(advertising the low-altitude flights), without his knowledge? He simply turned towards me and spread his arms outwards in a despairing gesture. He was indicating his total lack of comprehension that such a thing could have happened. I knew the feeling.*

Thus, I suppose, had Alice not met the white rabbit and fallen down a different hole to surface in the Antipodes, might Lewis Carroll have entitled his fairy tale, *The Adventures of Alice in Erebusland.* Unfortunately none of the judges who would be called on to examine the case would be enlightened by Lewis Carroll's sense of the absurd.

* * *

In the course of the inquiry Mahon and Baragwanath travelled to London, Washington and the Antarctic, examining the phenomenon of 'whiteout', checking and cross-checking other points at issue, and talking to experts.

In Washington they met officials of the US air traffic control base at McMurdo. Afterwards, when they flew to the Antarctic and visited the base themselves, they got their biggest surprise.

As a judge, Mahon was used to witnesses perjuring themselves. He expected untruths and evasions, and so was not unduly thrown at the Pentagon when he inquired about the flight-deck tapes which appeared to have been tampered with, and was unable to contact the officers who had been on duty at McMurdo on the day of the fatal flight. One of these had spoken by radio with the approaching DC10 minutes before it crashed. The Pentagon was unhelpful. Mahon and Baragwanath were politely but firmly fobbed off. Nor was Mahon taken aback on reaching McMurdo later to learn that his visit had been expected and that they, the personnel at the base, had been warned to stay mum. He was, however, unprepared to discover that when the first investigators arrived within days of the crash, they had been greeted with 'expressions of astonishment' on the part of McMurdo personnel, both Americans and New Zealanders, that none of the crew of the fatal flight had ever been to the Antarctic before.

'This was such an obvious precaution,' Mahon wrote, 'they could scarcely believe the verified fact that neither pilot on TE901 on November 28, 1979, had previously flown in the region.'

Here was a new element. It hinted at complicity in New Zealand between the airline and the Ministry of Civil Aviation, deepening Mahon's suspicions of a cover-up.

* * *

At this point I had better come clean and declare my own interest. When I first conceived this exercise about three men who fell foul of the establishment and/or whose lives were abbreviated by levels of stress largely not of their making, I decided to tell the stories where possible from the inside, in their words. It seemed a reasonable approach. They were men at the top of their profession whose integrity was not in doubt. Especially was this so in the case of Peter Mahon, who would write a report which would touch the moral conscience of a nation. It would also spell the end of his career — not, by a great irony, because he had done anything that was wrong, but because in exposing some of the fault-lines and hypocrisy at the base of our society he had done something that was right. Erebus is not a case set in stone. It is an argument. His report was an exceptional response to an exceptional chain of circumstances. Before it, Peter Mahon was unknown to the public at large; after it, he was a national figure.

His report remains controversial. It broke the rules of judicial behaviour. Those men who would destroy him were few, but they represented the judicial establishment in two countries, and they caught him on a point of law where he was vulnerable.

At issue, his critics said, was a question of bias or fair play — 'natural justice' or 'natural fairness' as it is now known. Another irony. (Mahon, to those who knew him, was natural justice personified.) His 'crime' was to accuse the management of a state institution of blatantly lying without giving it a chance to answer back — he had, in other words, 'exceeded his jurisdiction'. At issue, in Mahon's view, was a question of credibility. This had to do with his role as a commissioner, which his critics said he had misconceived; a case of the pot calling the kettle black — it was they who had exceeded their jurisdiction, not he, his.

When he was appointed Royal Commissioner, no manual existed to tell Mahon how to proceed, what he could or could not do, or could or could not say. He was free to conduct the inquiry in any way he wished. Any conclusions he reached on the evidence as to causation were within his powers. He had, as he saw it, one overriding task: to discover the truth.

There are several 'truths'. Mine is based in part on the book Mahon wrote shortly before he died, *Verdict on Erebus*. No one else talked to experts on three continents, plumbed the enigma of 'whiteout' and the navigational issue, pored over 284 documents and exhibits and sifted through 3000 papers after listening to evidence for 75 days. I make no apology for taking sides.

In his book, there is a chapter six pages long which he entitles 'The Anxieties of Mr Martin'. It concerns Mahon's and Baragwanath's visit to London. They flew to London somewhere about the ninth or tenth week, in November 1980, by which time an atmosphere of profound disbelief and mistrust had settled over the inquiry room in downtown Auckland. David Baragwanath's questioning of Air New Zealand's witnesses had revealed an organisation that was severely dysfunctional, its executives in denial. They had gone to London principally to discuss a transcript of the flight-deck tapes, one of the key matters in dispute, and had booked their return flight to New Zealand, when there was a confidential and urgent summons to meet a Mr Martin who represented the airline's insurance company in London. They met at the main office of Lloyd's underwriters. Peter Martin was an aviation law expert who did a great deal of work for Lloyd's. He had been following the transcripts of the hearings in Auckland, he said. His client was becoming alarmed, given the number and size of insurance claims that might be expected from the victims' families, at the case being presented to Mahon by Air New Zealand. It appeared to be crumbling. Was it so?

Mahon agreed it was so. The navigational evidence was in tatters, the suggestion that the aircrews were not permitted to descend below 16,000 feet had been destroyed inadvertently by one of its own witnesses; between them some 15 witnesses had committed a total of 47 blunders or omissions bearing on the disaster. However, having told Mr Martin that he disbelieved much of the evidence and might have to make a finding against Air New Zealand, Mahon added in his dry way that there was still time for the damage to be repaired — 'There was evidence still to be heard which might show that my current impression is wrong.' It was a coded warning, but an honourable one in the interests of fairness. In the end it was Lloyd's who would have to bear the costs. Mahon knew the warning would be passed on immediately, and he hoped it might have a salutary effect. Probably he was being naïve. The warning was indeed passed on by Mr Martin, both to Air

New Zealand and to Lloyd's brokers around the world, although with little apparent effect, Mahon says. To the end, the Air New Zealand management maintained its theme of 'pilot error'. Its basic position 'had not changed by so much as one iota'.

* * *

Mahon spent some weeks studying the evidence and writing up his report in Auckland, then went south to spend a few days with his son Sam in north Canterbury. There were some 3500 pages of evidence and judicial summings-up to sift through, much of it technical. The report was finally signed off and delivered in April 1981.

The Sunday before the report was due to be released on the Monday, Mahon, wrapped up in an old greatcoat, and Sam went duck shooting in the hills behind Waikari.

'A rare visit,' Sam writes. 'I remember the wind riffling the black pond and the restlessness of the trees. I remember him lighting a cigarette in the niche of his lapel, the shotgun broken in the crook of his arm ... "Tomorrow," he said, "all hell's going to break loose."' As indeed it did.

Mahon had expected that the directors of Air New Zealand would be angered by his findings; and that the airline would attack him publicly. Here at the end of his report (para 377) is the Commissioner's conclusion:

> *No judicial officer ever wishes to be compelled to say that he has listened to evidence which is false. He always prefers to say, as I hope the hundreds of judgments which I have written will illustrate, that he cannot accept the relevant explanation, or that he prefers a contrary version set out in the evidence. But in this case the palpably false sections of the evidence which I heard could not have been the result of mistake or faulty recollection. They originated, I am compelled to say, in a pre-determined plan of deception. They were very clearly part of an attempt to conceal a series of disastrous administrative blunders and so, in regard to the particular items of evidence to which I have referred, I am forced reluctantly to say that I had to listen to an orchestrated litany of lies.*

'Paragraph 377' came at the end of a report, 167 pages long, which was a thorough and comprehensive analysis of the evidence. It said that the pilots were the victims of a navigational blunder by the airline and a polar phenomenon called 'whiteout'. It overturned the findings of the chief air inspector of pilot error, and placed the blame squarely on the airline management. Besides exonerating the crew and charging Air New Zealand with irregularities and concerted attempts at deceit, Mahon ordered the airline to pay $150,000 towards the public cost of the inquiry.

The fallout was cataclysmic, the airline stunned. The storm unleashed in the press triggered a kind of public and political pandemonium, which polarised much of the country and extended to the highest levels. The prime minister was infuriated, and Mr Muldoon attacked the judge publicly. At first Muldoon seemed taken aback, commenting merely that 'it would have been better if Mr Justice Mahon had phrased his views less elegant and more precisely'; later, when the courts became involved, he took the offending (litany of lies) paragraph as a personal affront, demanding to know the source of the allegations ('Lies? Who lied? Where are their names?') and — a final insult — refusing to table the report in Parliament.

Still, the judge must have felt pleased at the overall popular response — he was voted in a national poll one of the ten most admired News Zealanders — besides vindicated. He had honoured his brief 'to inquire into and report his findings and opinions on the crash of the DC10'. He had condemned the airline certainly, but to do less — in the traditional manner of a judge in court saying that he found it hard to believe the evidence presented to him by the airline and that, in the absence of the crew, two pilots with exemplary records of thousands of hours of flying to their credit, he was not prepared to reach a finding that they had caused the disaster — would have been a cop-out. He could not. He felt compelled. He had a duty to perform. As he wrote later to a correspondent in Denmark, so obvious and overwhelming were the management errors and omissions indicating an organised plan of deception, that 'I really had no alternative.'[3]

He must have felt confident in his judgment, and safe, or at least safe from any retaliatory attack in open court by Air New Zealand, however bruised or wounded its management might be by his findings. He expected them to be angry, he tells us. We usually think of a Royal

---

3 'When all these errors and omissions are added together (and) you find that 15 airline officials, all highly skilled and intelligent, made a total of 47 errors and omissions. And it was contended that every one of these witnesses was acting independently of every other and was independently mistaken, I found myself unable to accept such a suggestion and would have come under public criticism had I done so.' (17 November 1981)

Commissioner as privileged, like an MP, immune to the threat of being put in the dock like an ordinary citizen. We tend to forget, if we think about it at all, how petty the Establishment can be, how personal and touchy besides powerful and vindictive, especially if the man at the top is a politician named Muldoon; how closely aligned Muldoon was with a cabal of friends with an almost manic interest in protecting the airline and its chief executive, Morrie Davis. Davis's attitude throughout, Mahon notes, was distinctly casual; he shrugged off his staff who were concerned at the cover-up, telling them privately, 'Don't worry, the government is behind us.'

At the end of his report to the Governor-General, summarising 'the causes of the disaster', Justice Mahon listed ten factors related to the pilot Jim Collins which preceded the occurrence of the disaster. If any one of these had not existed, he said, there would have been no disaster. He concluded that it was a result of a rare and malign set of circumstances, a million-to-one chance. At this stage the odds against the judge himself also becoming a victim of the crash must have seemed almost equally rare.

In the event Air New Zealand moved swiftly. It first rejected Mahon's report ('RANKS CLOSE AS REPORT REJECTED' ran a headline), then went to the Head of the

House, the prime minister. It is pertinent at this point to remember that Mr Muldoon, as Minister of Finance, was the airline's chief shareholder. So the airline went silent for about 48 hours, during which time, according to the record, the chief executive and others of the Air New Zealand board flew to Wellington for a two-hour meeting with the prime minister. It was then announced that the chief executive, Mr Davis, and Captain Ian Gemmell, the chief pilot, would begin a combined legal action seeking a judicial review of Mahon's findings in the High Court. It would be 'in the area of staff integrity', the board's chairman, a man named Mace, announced. It sounded strange.

Even stranger was a move by the judges of the Court of Appeal to wrest the proceedings from their High Court colleagues. Obviously, as Justice Speight and others insisted, it should go first to the High Court. The High Court, on the cab-rank principle, came first. In the event Speight was overruled, the lower court bypassed, with the application for review jumping the queue and going straight to the Court of Appeal. This was unfortunate for Mahon. In 1981 the Court of Appeal was presided over by the one man who, of all jurists in the country, was the one least likely to agree with Justice Mahon's findings. It was something he hadn't counted on.

* * *

Enter Sir Owen Woodhouse, pillar of the Establishment and one of the towering legal reformers of the age. Sir Owen was the president of the appellate court which ruled on Mahon's findings, and the author of the judgment which would initiate the chain of circumstances leading to Justice Mahon's ruin. It seems almost a crime to speak ill of such an eminent figure, author of the world's first no-fault accident compensation (ACC) scheme, a man known for his generosity and compassion, and a highly decorated war hero (into the bargain); to align him in company with the unpleasant chief of Air Zealand Morrie Davis, who declared, speaking of Mahon's report, 'I get pissed off when people laud the gentleman who, in terms of that determination, was incompetent.' Yet that is where the Woodhouse judgment of December 1982, effectively whitewashing the airline of any attempted cover-up, will place him.

Woodhouse was a protégé of Chief Justice Richard Wild. It was Wild who propelled him into the ACC hearings. When Owen Woodhouse joined the Bench in 1962, only one other judge, the former chief justice, Barrowclough, VC, DSO, had been decorated for war service. Woodhouse's early career and Mahon's were similar, two young men with formidable minds returning from the war each with a fine record, Woodhouse serving with motor torpedo boats in the Adriatic then with the partisans in Yugoslavia, Mahon with Battalion in Italy. Two busy young men, getting married, having children, taking up their interrupted law studies with diligence, grasp and a capacity for lateral thinking which would lead them in their separate ways to the High Court bench; one in Napier, the other, Mahon, in Auckland, where for a short time they overlapped. Then their ways diverged. Woodhouse, after making his name with the ACC report, moved to the Court of Appeal, where he was made a Privy Councillor and became known as a champion of social reforms and 'fairness'.

So much seems to hang on a good war. The war meant a great deal to Mahon, although he seldom spoke of it and didn't wear his RSA badge, his son says. Perhaps he had a chip on the shoulder; the award for gallantry which he allegedly declined was a relatively minor one, an MM (Military Medal), not an MC (Military Cross, which was awarded to officers only). Woodhouse, with his old-boy and particularly wartime connections — he was a gilded Lieutenant-Commander, DSO, in the navy — put him on a different perch to Mahon.

Woodhouse was in many ways more tolerant, certainly more liberal in his approach to the law than Mahon. A colleague, Duncan McMullin, cites a dissenting opinion where Woodhouse defended a man's right to commit suicide and thought that another man, a convicted murderer, should be allowed out to spend Christmas with his family. It speaks almost of an air of innocence, something 'soft', as with the famous English law reformer, Lord Denning.

There was nothing soft about Peter Mahon. His sometimes harsh sentencing of convicted criminals, especially for crimes against women, reportedly railroading the defendant as if prosecuting him, 'disgusted' Woodhouse; while at the other extreme, in his uprightness, Woodhouse frowned upon the element of comedy which entered some of Mahon's published judgments, as evidence of frivolity. An example being the case of two church ministers who attempted to cheat an elderly family retainer which came before Mahon in 1975. 'In the early part of 1973 two Auckland clergymen decided to beguile the tedium of ecclesiastical life by entering into the field of property speculation ... ' Justice Mahon's judgment begins (Haunui Investments and Owen Bambury, Minister of Religion, AND James Thomas, Minister of Religion).

Sir Owen Woodhouse was a very proper man. He did not lack humour or a sense of style ('Of course I know nothing at all about the subject,' he would interrupt an eager advocate in full flow — and then put to him an unexpected and devastating question which had the young barrister floored).

Possibly years of adulation and public recognition had given him a sense of invulnerability which made his probity and uprightness fair game for Mahon's sardonic wits and sense of the ridiculous. Neither man, it must be said, lacked an ego. (The word 'huge' in each case comes to mind.) And if, as seems likely, Woodhouse resented the widespread recognition of Mahon's 167-page document, its international acceptance and the fulsome praise being lavished upon it, then perhaps the element of professional jealousy — a grudging awareness that there was a rival in the room — was mutual.

* * *

My first indication Mahon had resigned from the Bench came in a roundabout way. I was driving. It was an autumn morning. I had the car radio on tuned to the National Programme. Sharon Crosbie was interviewing Judge

Mahon. I pulled off the road and turned up the volume. I listened, spellbound. I am not sure what it was that held me. It was not the judge's voice, which was slightly hesitant and in no way remarkable. I think it was a quality of fearlessness — did I even know the name Mahon then? (We were living in Jerusalem when the crash occurred, and subsequently were out of touch with events in New Zealand.) He spoke with a slight lisp. He exposed matters of general deceit and public interest, normally hidden by the mandarins of whichever branch of the Establishment wished to protect itself, or some other branch connected to it.

I think he ducked one question. He responded to another, about the prime minister, saying, 'I don't think he read the report', and made it plain that embedded in a small cabal of prime ministerial 'friends' in and around Air New Zealand were members of the legal hierarchy and the civil aviation division which had secretly waived the rules about altitude restriction. It was the first time I had heard anyone stand up to Mr Muldoon, and I now realise, in hindsight, it was probably this refusal to be intimidated and to flout the rules of the Establishment that so endeared Mahon to the public at large. Overnight he became a populist, not in any derogatory sense but as a man of the people.

The interview was broadcast on 1 February 1982. The Court of Appeal had delivered its findings in December, shortly before Christmas, and Mahon had resigned in protest a few days later. A majority decision of the Court of Appeal had ruled that a Royal Commissioner was not entitled to make adverse findings of credibility in his report to Parliament without the persons concerned being warned of his intention to do so. It also quashed his order that the airline pay $150,000 in costs. It was a severe rebuke, and a matter for resentment perhaps, but not resigning. Indeed Mahon's abrupt decision to hand in his ticket was more of a shock than the Court of Appeal's ruling, which later would be proved to be flawed and inaccurate.

At this stage, Air New Zealand was still telling a false tale, still pretending that it had done no wrong and shifting the blame onto the pilots for not having avoided the mountain which was in front of them. In the interview, Mahon spoke openly about a conundrum which I suspect few people understood, and which he said the Court had either ignored or failed to grasp, such as the absence of horizon and the freak light. It wasn't freak, he said; it was just that the briefing officers had omitted to warn the pilots that flat light or 'whiteout' was a common occurrence in polar regions. As the DC10 approached McMurdo Sound, air traffic control at McMurdo suggested that the plane descend through the cloud layer, which had a base of about 3000 feet, and then level out in clear air at 1500 feet, where visibility was unlimited. Or would have been, if the standard computer path the DC10 was locked onto had not been changed a few hours before, without telling the pilots, putting the DC10 on a collision course with the mountain. The aircraft would then have overflown Scott Base and McMurdo Base with landmarks in sight for 20 miles on either side, in accordance with ordinary procedure of Air New Zealand and Qantas scenic flights. The personnel at McMurdo Sound were well aware of the weather phenomenon in polar regions, whereby with a pale, solid, overcast sky and the unrelieved whiteness of the snow, the ground surface appears uniformly flat. At no stage would Mount Erebus have been visible to a crew that was 27 miles off-course. An aircraft crew in these conditions, flying in clean air, can fly directly into a snow slope without realising the ground is rising in front of them. This ocular illusion is described in arctic regions as 'flat light'.

It was a long interview. Mahon's surprise resignation was but a few days old. He had stepped down in an apparently retaliatory action which was a finite act. With the long summer holidays beginning, it was expected that the Erebus affair would cease to be of consuming interest and would quietly die down.

However I realised that the opposite was happening. He was defending his corner. He was fighting back, with half the country listening. He was on the attack. He would take his case to the Privy Council. OK, technically he had erred. He had broken one of the rules of fair play — *audi alteram partem* (hear the other side). But this, in the circumstances, was highly debatable. It was hardly a hanging matter. It was anyway Mission Impossible. He had already warned the airline specifically — once in chambers, and again through its London broker, Lloyd's — that he believed that witnesses were lying and intended to say so if they continued to falsify the facts.

For Mahon to comply to the letter with the rules of natural justice and express his disbelief in public would have meant risking the police filing proceedings in the High Court to stop the hearings, on the grounds of declared bias. (This was exactly what was happening at the time to the Australian judge, Mr Justice Taylor, in the Arthur Allan Thomas inquiry.) Perhaps Mahon wished he could reconvene the hearings, reopen the inquiry and, in a chapter-and-verse exercise on what is known as 'the Chilcot model', invite those witnesses he intended to criticise to respond either in person or in writing. What would have been their response? They would at once have wanted to refute the criticisms by calling other witnesses and/or demanding further investigations, which would have held up the inquiry for a lengthy period. The Sir John Chilcot report, set up to inquire into the United Kingdom's involvement in the Iraq war, is being published finally this week as I write (July 2016). It has taken seven years to get it into print.

No, no. Mahon was caught on the horns of a dilemma. In his estimation, he had already done enough by way of warning. You don't have to say to the oaf who has just raped your daughter, a legal friend reminds me, 'I must now give you the benefit of the rules of natural justice before I hand you over.' Of course, even criminals are given their rights on arrest!

What mattered most to Mahon was that the essence and guts of his investigation into the disaster — what caused it — remained intact, largely untouched. (No reputable body had criticised it or ever would.) He may have mentioned this.

At the end of the hour-long interview I sat up. It was as if I had been dreaming. The facts alone he had been recounting, evidence of a multitude of errors, such gross and unwavering improprieties, were mesmerising, doubly so when delivered in that hesitant, rasping voice. The interviewer said to him, 'Would you sit on another Royal Commission, if you were asked?' He considered this. 'Yes, I think so.' Then he added briskly, 'Yes. Why not?' There was a lift, a note of buoyancy in his voice. He sounded almost cheerful. Then why resign? the interviewer asked.

'Ah, that. That was the minority thing.'

One man, he said. Or she said.

'You mean Woodhouse. The Woodhouse judgment?'

'I had no grounds, he said. I don't believe in New Zealand's legal history that any Supreme Court or High Court judge has ever been told by a Court of Appeal that he has no grounds for a finding of credibility. Yes. The minority judgment.'

Sharon Crosbie, the interviewer, seemed to know what he was talking about. I was puzzled.

'No grounds, it said.'

'That was the finding that made me decide. It was the final straw. I thought to myself, "Right. I'm off." It was a public announcement.'

It was then that his tone changed. His voice until then had remained controlled and even, with an occasional sharp reply or contradiction, but no hint of anger. Now he was not just angry, he was outraged.

> Re, Erebus Royal Commission; Air New Zealand Ltd v Mahon (No. 2) *(October 1981) was perhaps the most emotionally fraught appeal heard by the Court of Appeal in its history. This was evident in the argument of the case and in the process by which the court fashioned its response. Significantly, while the court intended to produce a single combined judgment, there emerged two combined judgments.*
>
> *(from Peter Spiller,* History of the NZ Court of Appeal 1958–1996*)*

It had not happened before. There were five judges. Three, led by Robin Cooke, later Lord Cooke of Thorndon, formed a majority opinion that Judge Mahon had breached natural justice, but left the substance of Mahon's report intact; the other two judges formed a minority opinion, which was in effect the opinion of one man, Sir Owen Woodhouse, president of the court — 'the Woodhouse judgment' as it would come to be known. Woodhouse went further than the others and attacked Mahon personally, saying he had no probative evidence for criticising the conduct of airline officials. It amounted to a disguised approbation of the air accident inspector's (Chippendale's) report which totally exonerated Air Zealand.

There is a considerable literature on the Erebus affair. None of it pays tribute to the toxicity of Woodhouse's role, except in passing, and we learn of it only in a footnote in Spiller. Woodhouse had been skirmishing around the subject since the publication of the Mahon Report, and had decided to attack it before the hearing began. The wording is interesting. It was important to recall, he said in an interview in 1998, 'the innocent people' affected by Mahon's obsessive report. Hence his appropriately strong answer. Even those people who did not share Woodhouse's beliefs and background were usually captivated by his air of benevolence and courtly charm, and this streak of incomprehension and naïveté will come as a surprise to them. His use of the word 'innocents' will rub many, a reminder of the gulf that I believe still separates the two sides.

It is recorded that on the very last day of the Commission's hearings, discussing Chippendale's claim that the pilots were flying in cloud and did not know where they were, Woodhouse posed a rhetorical question: how could they have flown directly into the mountain when it was right there in front of them? At this point Mahon's counsel appearing for the Attorney-General, David Baragwanath, sighed and sat down.

The fervour and air of chaotic bewilderment that characterised the sitting were evident from the morning of day one, when Air New Zealand's counsel, Lloyd Brown, objected to the presence of Mahon's counsel, Baragwanath and Gary Harrison. Woodhouse, presiding, supported Brown. He refused them right of entry or audience at the hearing. There was a heated argument. The Solicitor General was sent for. In the end, Woodhouse, kicking the bench with his knee under the table, grudgingly agreed. 'All right, they can stay.'

At the end of the hearing some days later, the five judges apparently agreed in principle on the central issues. Woodhouse was deputed to write the major judgement.

* * *

The Woodhouse judgement explained my puzzlement during the radio interview with Sharon Crosbie. When he had suddenly snapped. It was clear during the interview that the majority judgment was something Mahon could have lived with. He was not personally humiliated. The Woodhouse judgment was a public pronunciation; it attacked Mahon's credibility, making it seem in the public eye that he was unable to distinguish truth from falsehood, at least that was how he took it. It left him compromised, with no option but to go to the Privy Council to try to repair the damage to his name.

He had sounded gung-ho about it in the broadcast. Insiders close to the Law Lords in London wrote to say he had a strong case. It was manifest during the radio broadcast that he had made the decision alone, without consulting widely; old friends like John Burn in Christchurch wondered if he was becoming clouded or obsessive. Mahon was driven by a turbulent ego, and popular opinion — he was bombarded by invitations — must have reinforced a feeling for the rightness of his cause, a feeling of invincibility. He could feel the current under him. He was in the stream of history now.

* * *

Enter Stuart Macfarlane. Senior lecturer, legal historian at the University of Auckland, student of satire, seriously unknown. In 1991, Stuart Macfarlane published a book, *The Erebus Papers*, which is 736 pages long. It has no index, weighs a ton, needs editing, is almost actionable, and it is brilliant.

Stuart Macfarlane says that he first became involved when he read the Court of Appeal's judgment in December

1981 and discovered a cardinal error. It suggested to him that Mahon's verdict was correct, and the court's, incorrect. Accordingly, he made the subject a research project, and after a period of prolonged labour — his wife says, 'he didn't come home to dinner for eight years' — produced *The Erebus Papers.* He urged Mahon not to go to London, saying he was making a fatal mistake. Mahon wouldn't listen.

Others like John Burn met the same resistance. 'There was always a shell,' Burn says. 'The long face, like a mask. There was a part of him I could never reach.'

One of his reasons for going to the Privy Council, Mahon told the government in his letter of resignation, was that the New Zealand Court of Appeal, in accusing him of being 'unfair', had misconceived the true nature of a Royal Commission which had no jurisdiction to interfere with the opinions expressed, which were not legal findings and which bound no one. Another reason was conflict of interest. The two judges who attacked him, Woodhouse and McMullin, had close personal ties with the airline: McMullin's son was a pilot, and Woodhouse's daughter worked in the Air New Zealand head office as a public relations officer. They should have recused themselves (stood down). Neither had done so.

In Macfarlane's view the Privy Council would judge him on a solitary point of law, natural justice. Writing in a Christchurch newspaper, *The Press*, Stuart Macfarlane pointed out to Mahon that, whatever happened, he was bound to be defeated. On at least three issues the Privy Council was bound to reject the appeal — and, further, that its ruling would not be affected by whether the Commissioner's claim of a predetermined plan of deception and lies was correct or not. Even if those remarks were true and the Privy Council believed they were true, the appeal would still be dismissed on the only relevant view, namely the law. This is, of course, what would happen.

Mahon wouldn't listen.

It took courage. He must at some point have been assailed by doubts and begun to nurse hidden fears that he was backing a lost cause.

In 1982, Mahon became ill. In the autumn of 1982 he wrote a letter to his sister in Christchurch, describing a shag he had seen on the edge of the tide at Diamond Harbour or Lyttelton: 'I envied that bird. He only knew the enemies which instinct, as opposed to intelligence, taught him to fear.'

* * *

The Privy Council's ruling was delivered in October 1983, nearly four years after the crash occurred. It is a strange, convoluted document. Having gone out of their way to praise the Commissioner 'for his brilliant and painstaking investigative work' — an investigation they call 'masterly' — the five Law Lords manage to discredit and blacklist him, while at the same time absolving both Air New Zealand and the pilots of blame. For this we have to thank Stuart Macfarlane. He dismembers the Privy Council document piece by piece.

If I read him right, the Privy Council has one overall aim: to protect the Establishment (the New Zealand government, judiciary, state airline, and civil aviation authority) against which the significance of Mahon's discoveries in the course of his inquiry, with their universal application to future management and accident safety procedures everywhere, is but of secondary importance. Macfarlane is disturbed by what he calls the Privy Council's 'economies with the truth'. This he demonstrates by listing some twenty-seven errors and misstatements, stitching them in quietly to show how they bear on facts as if facts themselves. He has a nice turn of phrase. He is obviously enjoying himself:

> *'The Privy Council wrongly claimed the Judge overlooked paragraph 1.17.7 of the Chippendale Report ...*
>
> *The Privy Council wrongly claimed the Judge was mistaken in alleging ...*
>
> *The Privy Council, like the Court of Appeal, failed to understand ...*
>
> *The Privy Council wrongly asserted that [the Chippendale paragraph] made crystal clear ... '*

I am getting ahead of myself here. But it helps to appreciate Macfarlane's method, and what for the most part he is about. Just as disturbing (he says) in such a random scattering of error and distortions, where you would expect a distribution with some in the judge's favour but others not, is the discovery that without exception these errors are to Mahon's detriment. How is this possible? Is it an accident? If the latter is the case, it seems to have required on the part of all five Law Lords 'a high degree of incompetence'. If it is deliberate, the following scenario suggests itself: faced with what it sees as a naïve colonial judge, the Privy Council has decided to remind him of his unspoken duty to the Establishment in New Zealand. This must mean that the Privy Council has decided to leave the neutrality of the sidelines and enter the fray itself, finding as facts that no 'orchestration of lies' has ever existed, thus clearing the airline management of any blame whatsoever.

Difficult to bring off? Not really. 'Again [Macfarlane says] the Privy Council rose to the occasion, this time with a twofold argument (707).' Moments later, he demonstrates an even more difficult feat of juggling it needs to perform. The problem, as ever, was Chippendale, the ubiquitous air accident inspector who seems to enjoy his role as the high priest of darkness in the eye of the pilots whom he blamed for everything.

Chippendale himself was an Establishment figure, and also posed a difficulty for the playwright Greg McGee who wrote a mini-series for television about the disaster, *Erebus: The Aftermath*. McGee, like Stuart Macfarlane, is astonished that the Privy Council should attempt to reconcile the irreconcilables in order to clear the various Establishment figures, and agrees with him that the Law Lords constructed a fantasy world that had never existed. Whose work to read? McGee's? Macfarlane's? Read both.

As to how to present the Privy Council's warped views and inconsistencies to his television audience, McGee sets a scene in the Mahons' garden where a worn-down, ailing judge explains to his wife:

> *The Privy Council is simply saying: one, that my analysis of the cause of the accident is brilliant and correct; two, that my analysis of the cause of the accident is incorrect, insofar as I give any weight to executive knowledge of low flying; three, that the Air New Zealand executives might well have been lying about their knowledge of low flying; four, that that doesn't matter because their Lordships don't consider low flying had anything to do with the disaster; and five, that because at the time they lied, the executives thought low flying was the cause of the disaster, it was quite understandable for them to want to lie.*

At the end of its ruling, the Privy Council suggested to the judge a kind of *quid pro quo*. In his 1981 report, Mahon absolved the pilots. Now in its 1983 ruling, the Privy Council had made what it considered a giant concession to Justice Mahon in supporting his action clearing the pilots, thus directly contradicting its own position towards Air New Zealand. The Privy Council had been generous. In return would the judge not like to join ranks and call it a day?

> *Their Lordships* [the Privy Council ruling ended] *cannot close this lengthy judgment without expressing their conviction that the time has now come for all parties to let bygones be bygones so far as the aftermath of the Mt Erebus disaster is concerned.*

It may have been the fatuity of remarks like this, belittling the grief of the families of the aircrew and the other 237 passengers who died, that initially roused Stuart Macfarlane. Why, yes, one or two witnesses might have perjured themselves. Yes, indeed. They might have emitted a couple of false notes while on oath. But if so they had done so as soloists, not in chorus. There had been no concerted plan or conspiracy. An occasional falsehood was but a manifestation of human fallibility and 'easy to understand and excuse'.

Their lordships concluded: 'The time has surely come by now for them to be allowed to be forgotten.' It was a coded signal for the judge to depart in dignified silence. Put up and shut up. (Thank God he didn't. He would not have written *Verdict on Erebus*.) But by then the damage was done. Peter Mahon's legal career was finished.

* * *

He was down but not out — in the cricketing analogy, 'still a strong runner'. He found he had a life again, and, until he became very ill and was forbidden from taking even the forbidden cigarettes, he was starting to become once more — even more so — what he had always been, a hero to the younger generation of practitioners and lawyers. The Auckland Bar, unlike the Bench, was not weevilled by those who sniffed at his popularity, an ability to attract a circle by merely enlarging on a point of law. On the final day of his career as a judge, it gave him a Bar dinner — with a record turnout. Four hundred attended.

Even the supermarket had its moments. Being retired, he discovered, was a strange status. He wrote to his friend, John Burn, 'Occasionally I join Mrs. M on a visit to the supermarket, a thing I have never done before ... A most instructive appearance. And the great thing is you can't leave without paying. Presiding at the meat sector was an old Army friend, Corporal Welsford, a genial and corpulent figure. When I had last seen the Corporal he was lying on the cobble-stones of the main square in Arezzo, with two bullet holes in his chest, but he assured me that he had made a good recovery and would be available at any time to select for me the choicest steaks in the supermarket armoury.'

Stuart Macfarlane's book *The Erebus Papers* serves, as he says, a dual purpose. It is about a particular aircraft crash. But its subject is also the application of justice and a reluctance by judges to articulate principle over practice, illustrated by their descent in Wellington and London into an academic fantasy world called Erebusland. An irony being that one of the judges, elevated to the highest perch on the appellate bench and having become a noted reformer, should be in need of reform himself; and that two men who in their separate ways raised the esteem of the judiciary in the public eye should end up competing with and fighting each other. Envy, of course, can be a form of praise, besides a kind of spur. There it is. Woodhouse and Mahon. But there is a good side.

'If I have learned anything from my father at all,' Sam Mahon says, 'it is an obstinate refusal to back down in the face of adversity.' Mahon had made a fatal error by going to London on appeal. (In fact, he had been too ill to travel. Margarita had gone in his stead.) He had been humiliated and effectively struck off. Now he knew pleasure. He turned to writing.

* * *

Mahon went back to Christchurch and wrote his book, *Verdict on Erebus*. He wrote it in three months. It seemed, Margarita says, to pour out of him.

Verdict on Erebus is an important book. It was an unashamed act of self-justification. It remains, nonetheless, an important book. It has a measured judicial tread. It reveals a man in a trance, in part still in shock, yet sure of himself. It reads like a thriller. It dismantles the Chippendale Report. It exposes the arrogance and contempt of airline officials to the Royal Commission itself. It gives the lie to those in the Woodhouse camp who describe the author as 'confused', a man 'out of his depth', who had gone 'seriously off the rails', and whose findings were 'utterly unsupportable'. And it gave a clear, comprehensive explanation of events to the families and relatives of those who died, helping to mend wounds still suppurating from the tragedy.

Predictably, the political and legal establishments took umbrage, criticising the book as an act of self-praise by a disgruntled litigant. Not only peers, but some of Mahon's friends were affronted. Judges, bound by judicial constraints, simply do not enter into debates or write books of this kind even in semi-retirement.

In 2008 Duncan McMullin, now Sir Duncan, in his memoir *A Lawyer's Tale* published a rebuttal of the Mahon Report. He said:

> *One may wonder how Mahon came to make the extravagant and utterly unsupportable findings on conspiracy that he did. I can only surmise that in giving expression to his literary talents, he overlooked some evidence or placed an erroneous, perhaps sinister, interpretation on what he heard. And with the weight of evidence he had to consider, he became confused as to the identity of the participants and the part they played.*

Alongside which we might set the final two paragraphs of *Verdict on Erebus*. Mahon wrote:

> *By a navigational (computer) error for which the aircrew was not responsible and about which they were uninformed, an aircraft had flown not into McMurdo Sound but into Lewis Bay, and there the elements of nature had so combined, at a fatal coincidence of time and place, to translate*

an administrative blunder in Auckland into an awesome disaster in Antarctica.

Much has been written about the weather hazards of Antarctica, and how they may combine to create a spectacular but hostile terrain but for my purposes the most definitive illustration of those hidden perils was the wreckage which lay on the mountainside, showing how the forces of nature, if given the chance, can sometimes defeat the flawless technology of man. For the ultimate key to the tragedy lay here, in the white silence of Lewis Bay, the place to which the airliner had been unerringly guided by its microelectronic navigational system, only to be destroyed in clear air and without warning, by a malevolent trick of the polar light.

* * *

Merely to write *Verdict on Erebus* was an act of courage, besides defiance. Three years earlier, when he had charged the airline with conspiring to deceive, Mahon had done so with the protection of his office. A Royal Commissioner could not be sued for defamation. Now, no longer a judge, he repeated the allegations — 'A pre-determined plan of deception ... an orchestrated litany of lies' — word for word as a private citizen effectively inviting Air New Zealand and those officials he had allegedly defamed, to sue him in open court. No one did.

After *Verdict on Erebus* won a major literary award, came a long short story, 'The Sniper', and another book, *Dear Sam*. The last publication was a collection of letters to his family, written by a man his daughter describes as 'contained', who had difficulty expressing his emotions, but now revealed himself in a full flowering of decency and an unsuspected warmth of heart. And wit, of course ('It was the sense of humour I married,' Margarita says). Writing was a hidden yearning. 'He had always wanted to write,' Sam says.

After returning to Christchurch where he had grown up and his career had begun, Mahon applied to his alma mater, the University of Canterbury, for a job. 'I should have no difficulty in getting a part-time job at Canterbury University,' he wrote to Bryan Todd, 'with the probability of becoming a professor in law later in the year, giving me time to write my book.' He was being over-optimistic. According to Sam, not only did the law school not appoint him when he applied, it did not even bother to reply to his letter of application. If true, such a put-down, astonishing as it may seem, was a barometer of a wider ostracism. Old friends deserted him; former colleagues like Ted Somers and Clint Roper disappeared into the judicial benchwork. Justice Clint (Sir Clinton) Roper had known Mahon in the war. He was an old hunting mate, a tall, jesting man with a booming voice. He and Mahon got on famously. They had served together on Italy. Roper became ill, and on the voyage home Mahon looked after his friend, who returned mentally scarred. Subsequently, when Clint was back on his feet, Mahon introduced him to the law. George Barton QC has recorded that, after Erebus, Mahon came upon Roper one day in the Cashmere Hills, walking on the other side of the road. 'Clint saw him, and looked away.'

We should not be surprised, I suppose. Betrayal, as Sam says, is sometimes more dependable than friendship.

It is an exaggeration to say that New Zealand has instinctively neutralised those men and women who have attempted to foist moral greatness on their country. We seem nonetheless to have gone about it in a regular and discriminating manner, second only perhaps to Italy. Luigi Barzini in his book *The Italians* gives us a long list of Italian dissenters who were persecuted or sent into exile because they upset the Establishment: Giambattista Vico, Galileo Galilei, Dante Alighieri, Giuseppe Mazzini. Some, like Tommaso Campanella, spent most of their lives in dungeons. 'A few of the worthiest were killed amid the rejoicing of the populace, burnt at the stake like Giordano Bruno and Savonarola, hanged like the patriots of the Neopolitan Republic in 1799, stabbed and stoned by the crowd like Cola di Rienzo.'

The New Zealand list is a little less lurid than Barzini's, but it is only marginally less comprehensive. It includes scientists, historians, lawyers, prophets, thinkers, philosophers, and ranges from William Pember Reeves in the 1890s to the artist Frances Hodgkins, the writer James Courage, the atom scientist Rutherford, the 'heretic' Lloyd Geering, the sinophiles Rewi Alley and James Bertram, the lawyer Jeremy Pope, the poets A.R.D. Fairburn and James K. Baxter ... marginalised, neutered, ignored, forgotten by their compatriots, or sent into exile for having deviated in some way from the norm. And among them, the late Honourable Justice Peter Thomas Mahon, more honourable than most.

* * *

He was never honoured in the civil list, although there was a flurry of petitions to the Government for a knighthood. Among them was a petition in 1984 signed by 48 prominent New Zealanders, among them a future Governor-General, Sir Anand Satyanand, and a future Chief Justice, Sian Elias. They spoke of the mercurial brilliance of Mahon's judgments from the Bench, his blend of honesty and fair play, his encouragement by example to a younger generation of lawyers, and, above all, his integrity and principle which had lifted the image of the judiciary in the public eye. Sir David Baragwanath, who was president of the United Nations Special Tribunal for Lebanon between 2010 and 2015, reminded the Lange Government of Mahon's service in Italy as a frontline infantryman; Richard Sutton, dean of the University of Otago's Faculty of Law wrote that, without Mahon's pioneering analysis, 'it must be doubtful whether the true causes (of the Erebus crash) would have been revealed'; Sian Elias spoke of his retirement from the Bench as a tragic and 'incalculable' loss. All to no avail.

It should have been a shoo-in. It is normal practice for retiring High Court judges of seniority to be knighted.

'Waste of time,' Peter Mahon had told his wife when the idea was put to him. 'I don't want it.' 'It's not for you,' Margarita said, 'it's the people, the people want it.' Eventually she said he relented and allowed his name to go forward. 'Nothing will come of it,' he said.

At the time, Prime Minister David Lange was out of the country, and the decision fell to his deputy, Geoffrey Palmer, who was Attorney-General. Palmer said no.

It would take almost 20 years before the Mahon Report, commissioned by the government, would be tabled in the House, in 1999. It was thought at the time that this would correct an injustice, and that the tabling of the Mahon Report would lead to its replacing the former and thoroughly discredited Chippendale Report. This, however, did not happen. It seems that the two contradictory reports continue to rate equally with the International Civil Aviation authorities.

* * *

While in Christchurch, Mahon had developed heart failure, a recurrence of a condition he had known as a young man. A painful sinus tumour was also diagnosed, and drug therapy treatment started. Back in Auckland, where he had picked up some part-time work teaching at the University of Auckland's Faculty of Law, he seemed to rally. However, his heart condition worsened, limiting what he could do and ruling out what should have been a simple operation on his cheek after the sinus tumour was identified. Radiotherapy sessions followed but proved excessive, stinging the mouth and leading to weeks of agony and a slow recuperation and apparent remission. At this time, he would sneak off with a twinkle in the eye to the TAB to put a few bets on — a reversion to his old habits as a newly appointed judge when he laboured hard to create time in the afternoon for a round of golf at Middlemore.

He was travelling between the hospital and the university lecture room almost to the end: old but not elderly, slightly stooped, greying, shrunken, emaciated yet still somehow distinguished, his voice without a microphone reduced to a whisper. He was lecturing on ethics and advocacy. The topic of his final lecture was 'Decency in Law'. Janet, his daughter, sat at the back of the room holding a glass of water to moisten his lips if he needed it. When he had finished, the students stood up and gave him an ovation.

Besides lecturing part-time at the university in Auckland, he conducted an inquiry into the 1984 Queen Street riots, and assisted with claims by Vietnamese veterans affected by the defoliant Agent Orange. In New York in 1986, tidying up work on the Agent Orange Trust, he collapsed and was rushed to hospital after a heart attack brought on by lugging a suitcase too far. He recovered and was sent home, even though the Christchurch *Star* was already featuring him on their obituary list.

'Wishful thinking,' he joked to John Burn. Three weeks later he was dead.

* * *

He died on 11 August 1986, aged 62. Former lawyer David Lange was prime minister. When Sir Owen Woodhouse died in 2014, he held an ONZM (Order of New Zealand Merit) and was widely regarded as one of the greatest living New Zealanders. Upon hearing news of his death, Parliament interrupted proceedings and Members stood for a minute's silence to honour his passing; tributes were read out from judges up and down the land. On the occasion of Peter Mahon's funeral service in Auckland nearly 20 years earlier, the Holy Trinity Cathedral in Parnell was packed. The tributes were no less fulsome but were rather more personal, and intimate; less judicial in tone. His peers, the judges, stayed away.

Well-known member of the legal fraternity, Bernard Brown, remembers two judges who were there; somebody else remembers three. Margarita Mahon said she counted four. This, when there were a lot of senior jurists and judges living in Auckland at the time.

Peter Mahon is possibly the only judge New Zealand has produced who became a legend in his lifetime. He matters because he did two things. One was practical: he wrote a report of world significance. It shifted the focus of travel accident investigation — especially air travel — for all time, the equivalent of a small revolution. Two: he showed us something of ourselves which we didn't know was there. I am talking of dissent. I am talking of maturity and the element of anarchy mentioned at the start of this book. While Mahon's place in history is assured, his value, however, is still undecided. He made no lasting impression on the law; rather, he defied it. He left the law no more and no less rigid than he found it. But in his stand for truth and justice against the craven reactionaries of the Establishment, he may have set a marker leaving New Zealand a more grown-up place where dissent was recognised and, for the first time, becoming cherished.

He is both folk hero and legend. His name has outlived that of those who discredited him — ten judges, five on the Court of Appeal in New Zealand, five on the Privy Council in London. These men possessed educated minds; they were highly civilised and courteous, they knew the world, they did not lack a sense of humour. Yet they were out of touch. They believed that they were upholding the law, but forgot about mercy. They forgot that justice without mercy is no justice at all. They espoused the littleness of small things and forgot the 257 people who died on the ice. In law, they were no doubt technically correct; morally, in their cynicism and indifference to the dead, they could not have been more wrong.

* * *

I am reminded of a plaque I saw near Berlin. Inscribed on a memorial plaque inside the Brandenburg-Görden penitentiary on the River Havel just west of Potsdam, where 1722 men and women who opposed Hitler and the Nazi regime were imprisoned and executed in the war years between 1940 and 1945, I read the words Zum Tode geführt — und siehe, wir leben ('Led to death — but see, we are alive').

In exceeding his brief, if that is what he did, Justice Peter Thomas Mahon may have upset his legal colleagues. But in the history of the law he joins a select few, like Justice Horton of Alabama, who had the courage to follow their conscience, even though they knew it might spell the end of their career.

Fiat justitia ruat caelum runs the Latin phase: 'Let justice be done, though the heavens fall.' The heavens did fall. Peter Mahon was a man destroyed. But, see, he lives.

Epilogue

In Sir James' long life in newsprint and books he stamped on his writing the staples of authority and clarity. A vital element of each is relevance and he made a fetish of that. The idea of *Breaking Ranks* had been with him for years, as had the singular careers of his friend Dr Saxby and Brigadier General Miles. In my hearing, someone said to James, 'Go for a triad; [X.] rebelled against society and, like them, suicided.' In a flash of impatience James shot back, 'I'm not looking for that. The theme is being at odds with the particular establishment and taking it on.' It cleared the air. 'Peter Mahon's the one. He's got to be.'

An irresistible choice. Those who had recommended Mahon to the Erebus commission appointment, in good old Kiwi style were looking for the safe pair of hands. A particular prime minister could recall the Tangiwai disaster and its tame conclusion avoiding institutional inadvertence: Mahon was thought to be the man for the job. How wrong, in that sense, was that judgment.

Besides alarming the establishment these three men had much in common. Each reached an apex in his vocation. The vocations were honourable ones. Each in his own way was a reformer and was articulate in speech and in writing about it. Like most folks, who don't get books written about them, they had their flaws. Very human, even engaging. Without them, theirs might not have been exceptional, recordable, lives. The nature of Mahon's death was different: he died of a disease that claims many of us. If Erebus was to prove his Waterloo it was also his apogee. (James found that signally challenging. So would William Shakespeare.) Peter Mahon could have scribed a ho-hum report noting pilot error in freakish weather. No party, except crew widows and families, would have been exceptionally offended. He could have seen out his time on the Bench and retired with a knighthood. Instead he did what he perceived to be his duty, declared some witnesses liars and others orchestrators of those lies. He went for the coordinates error (the jugular) as *causa causans*. In a blaze of publicity he resigned the Bench.

The last few years — even as a kind of popular hero (and perhaps partly due to that) — were uncomfortable ones.

There was about the older Reginald Miles an element of self-torture. Even after his derring-do escape he expressed anxiety over a possible (improbable) court martial. Earlier, in the desert, instead of boldly brandishing a rifle at Rommel's tanks, he, senior staff-officer, might have been expected to seek the haven of HQ. He would, in captivity, have agonised over the long wait for his superior's ('understanding') letter and, after it, over its every starchily succinct word. (Freyberg, unlike Miles, was no empathetic communicator.)

Passionate for reform of psychiatric institutions, Dr John Saxby read the writing on the walls he was bringing down. The incipient neo-liberal regime, which he feared, might prove workable but only at a gigantic taxpayer expense. Skimping, he foresaw, would bring human disaster. And his own reforms, with his career, would (as he saw it) amount to no more than an historical footnote.

The flaws or foibles of these men were minor compared to their strengths. The former certainly contributed to their breaking ranks. The psychiatrist could see no way a different (cost-cutting) medical regime could accommodate his talents or his philosophy.

The gunnery strategist chose to be with the *hoi polloi*, outflanked, overrun but mixing it with the Hun. In cold anger the Royal Commissioner reached for a phrase that would define yet effectively end his legal career. All three were brave — noble even — in their own styles yet perhaps momentarily foolhardy. A bit bloody-minded. Unlike their peers, the survivors — and James McNeish calls out the registers on them — they were the risk-takers. If a difference marked off Mahon from the other two, it was the blaze of public interest in which he broke with the establishment (and by that word I mean the political rather more than the judicial one).[4]

Oddly, the psychiatrist could have accounted for Reg Miles's death by tapping Émile Durkheim: the concomitant of sudden exultation can be dramatic despair? John Saxby's own end may be more difficult to explain. McNeish's earlier work *Mr Halliday and the Circus Master* may assist the keen inquirer.[5]

Justice Mahon did not go to his death without recriminations. He was offended by some arch treatment over Monte Cassino. (I could see no reason why a promotion was offered as an alternative to a decoration.) As one

4 Though here and there there may have been a tad of overlapping.

5 Durkheim, É., *Suicide*.

who took pride in his courtroom work as a detector of untruths,[6] he died convinced that his identification at the Erebus hearing of a 'predetermined plan of deception', of 'lies' — and 'orchestrated' ones at that — was beyond question. A considerable mystery surrounds his omission to permit his alleged 'liars' and 'orchestrators' to answer for themselves to the Commission. These resounding phrases would long outrun the occasion but so would the spectre of neglected natural justice.[7]

Some of the judicial brethren were dismayed at his decision to publish *Verdict on Erebus* after resigning from the Bench. Any such exercise bearing so directly on a controversial career matter is by convention frowned upon. The former judge may well have justified the book as the only means of expressing 'his side' of the matter after

6 He told me he preferred judge-only trials to trials by jury.

7 Judges of the Court of Appeal in Wellington made much of 'the language' including the alleged 'stance' of Air New Zealand in a finding of 'excess of jurisdiction'. In London the Privy Council sidestepped that but agreed with Wellington there was a breach of natural justice. The Privy Council noted 'some falsehoods' in a few of Air New Zealand witnesses' testimony but insufficient to warrant the Commissioner's words of reproof. As an old judge once told me it is the actual adjudicator who sees and hears the witnesses and who is in the best seat to remark who does or does not squirm under examination. Both reviewing bodies made a concession to that but added that distance can lend objectivism.

the judgments of the New Zealand Court of Appeal and the Privy Council in London. Sir James McNeish with his fetish for relevance might have seen it as another — the final — act of breaking ranks.[8]

* * *

James lived the lives of these men in the last years of his own. He used me as a kind of sounding board only when he felt he lacked direct experience of, say, mischievous 'cod' poetry and, as he deftly put it, 'one's reaction to being under fire'. I had penned a verse or two for *Mr Halliday* and James knew I had been shot at in the 'Malaya Emergency'. My reply was that, unlike his three brave subjects, especially Miles in two wars, I was a coward and, had I been wearing a white shirt, not a khaki one, I would have waved it at the enemy. But I couldn't see an enemy or even guess at its motivation. 'That, dear Bernard, is not cowardice,' he replied. 'It's puzzlement.'

8 A modern deviation from convention occurs in an article by Lord Hope in Oliver (ed.) *Justice, Legality and the Rule of Law* (2009) where his lordship criticises the judgment by Lord Hoffmann in *Christian and Others v The Queen* (Pitcairn Island) [2006] UKPC 47, a case in which Lord Hope was also a member of that body.

Good old Jim. He always shone the best light on those who lacked his own great moral gumption and strength of mind. And he showed that repeatedly in the field research and writing of his many books.

Bernard Brown, Parnell.
A friend.

PICTURES

Photograph of John Saxby (page 5) © Frizby Smith, 1983.

Photograph of Reginald Miles (page 111), courtesy National Army Museum, New Zealand (2003.305).

Photograph of Peter Mahon (page 209), courtesy Sam Mahon. Portrait of Peter Mahon taken before publication of *Verdict on Erebus*, 1984. (George Weigel and Son)